D0976007

"*The Eternal Current* is an impassioned call to move beyond spiritual observation into divine participation. Jesus didn't invite us to simply believe about the River of God; he invited us to swim! By learning from the perennial wisdom of the wide Christian community, Aaron has written a book that will launch you in your practice from the transcendent to the particular, and it will draw you in your faith perspective from the particular to the transcendent."

—FR. RICHARD ROHR, founder of the Center for Action and Contemplation and author of *Falling Upward*

"*The Eternal Current* is a gift, challenge, cure for what ails, and blessing. Rather than simply pointing to the problem, Aaron has put in the time and energy to craft a new way forward, not only for you as an individual but also for your faith community. This book will cause you to reimagine a life-giving, hopeful, centered, embodied, and *living* path to follow Jesus."

—SARAH BESSEY, author of *Out of Sorts* and *Jesus Feminist*

"Aaron Niequist has written the defining account of a generation of evangelicals who are disenchanted with the often shallow wells of evangelical spirituality and who are looking for a deeper, more robust, transformational expression of their faith. What sets his story apart, however, is that he stayed within his native tribe to contend for a different kind of space. *The Eternal Current* is the new construction on the other side of the deconstruction, written not by a theorist but by a practitioner."

—JONATHAN MARTIN, author of *How to Survive a Shipwreck* and *Prototype*

"You hold in your hand a brilliant exploration of those ancient but evergreen practices the church must recover to remain a vital and prophetic presence in the world. This field-tested and practical guide will equip and empower you to live in and lead others into the life-giving waters of a practice-based faith."

—Ian Morgan Cron, author of *The Road Back to You*

"I am inspired by Aaron Niequist's bold vision of a church that is open to learning from all the branches of our Judeo-Christian tradition. Aaron has documented one of the most refreshing approaches to practice-based discipleship that I have ever encountered."

—Fr. J. Michael Sparough, SJ, Bellarmine Jesuit Retreat House

"For far too long we have wrongly equated depth of knowledge with depth of life when it comes to our discipleship. I'm so grateful Aaron Niequist has presented a creative vision for us to reimagine life with God. Our churches and we as individuals desperately need to swim with this Eternal Current of practice-based faith."

—Rich Villodas, lead pastor of New Life Fellowship, New York

"I value this book because of Aaron's winsome way of inviting us to swim in the Eternal Current of God's kingdom by engaging in the life-giving practices spiritual seekers have used through the ages to open themselves to God. And what a clear and compelling invitation it is, emerging from his own life and witness! I share Aaron's vision for practice-based communities that learn together how to swim in the deep end of the pool for the sake of others, and I am glad we have taken the deep dive together."

—Ruth Haley Barton, author of *Sacred Rhythms*

"This book is for all of us who want to discover how to grow deeper roots in loving God and our neighbor in the radical way Jesus described in the Gospels—through the rhythms of grace found in practices of public worship."

—David M. Bailey, coauthor of *Race, Class, and the Kingdom of God* study series

AARON NIEQUIST

THE ETERNAL CURRENT

How a Practice-Based Faith Can Save Us from Drowning

WATERBROOK

THE ETERNAL CURRENT

Details in some anecdotes and stories have been changed to protect the identities of the persons involved.

Hardcover ISBN 978-0-7352-9116-4
eBook ISBN 978-0-7352-9117-1

Cover design by Kristopher K. Orr; cover photograph by Eric Niequist, New Branch Films

Published in the United States by WaterBrook, an imprint of the Crown Publishing Group, a division of Penguin Random House LLC, New York.

WATERBROOK® and its deer colophon are registered trademarks of Penguin Random House LLC.

Library of Congress Cataloging-in-Publication Data
Names: Niequist, Aaron, author.
Title: The eternal current : how a practice-based faith can save us from drowning / Aaron Niequist.
Description: First edition. | New York : WaterBrook, an imprint of the Crown Publishing Group, a division of Penguin, [2018]
Identifiers: LCCN 2018000555| ISBN 9780735291164 (hardcover) | ISBN 9780735291171 (electronic)
Subjects: LCSH: Christian life.
Classification: LCC BV4501.3 .N54 2018 | DDC 248.4—dc23
LC record available at https://lccn.loc.gov/2018000555

Printed in the United States of America
2018—First Edition

10 9 8 7 6 5 4 3 2 1

SPECIAL SALES
Most WaterBrook books are available at special quantity discounts when purchased in bulk by corporations, organizations, and special-interest groups. Custom imprinting or excerpting can also be done to fit special needs. For information, please email specialmarketscms@penguinrandomhouse.com or call 1-800-603-7051.

To Shauna and the boys. You three are the center of the center of the center. Let's swim together forever.

Contents

Introduction

The Eternal Current

A great and mighty River flows throughout history toward the healing and restoration of all things. If you have read the Bible, you know how the story ends: love conquers death, a new heaven and earth are established, and the God of love and justice finally puts all things to rights. Our Creator is carrying every corner of creation into a beautiful future.

Jesus Christ referred to this River as the kingdom of God, a realm where the things that God wants to happen happen "on earth as it is in heaven" (Matthew 6:10). Jesus explained it as "good news to the poor . . . freedom for the prisoners . . . recovery of sight for the blind," freedom for the oppressed, and God's favor on earth (Luke 4:18–19). Or as Dr. Martin Luther King

Jr. taught, "The arc of the moral universe is long, but it bends toward justice."[1]

You and I have been invited to swim with this Eternal Current for the sake of the world. Jesus didn't merely invite us to believe about the River. He didn't say, "Here is the truth. Believe me." He declared, "I am the truth. Follow me." Beliefs are important, but they're not nearly enough. The invitation is to wade into the River and swim.

This really is good news. Swimming with Christ is the *way* to embrace the *truth* of the abundant *life* that Jesus taught about. And the Eternal Current will carry us into the joy of getting swept up in God's work of redeeming and restoring all things.

Yet so many of us miss the invitation. We concentrate on perfecting our beliefs but never step into the water. Or we decide to swim but get stuck in the comfort and safety of the shallows.

Friend, I missed this invitation for years. I believed Christian ideas, prayed Christian prayers, and attended Christian events, but I never learned to swim with Christ in the River of God. Though I had been a Christian since childhood, I missed out on the passion, meaning, peace, and power of eternal life. I traded the richness of swimming in the River for the dry riverbank of religion. Honestly, I still wash up onto these rocks from time to time.

But Christ keeps inviting me (and you) back into the Eternal Current. Over and over, through the mundane and the dramatic details of our lives, in deeply religious and wildly profane moments alike, through heartbreak and delight and confusion and epiphany, Christ continues to gently reach out to us.

Few sections of Scripture capture this better than Eugene Peterson's poetic articulation of Matthew 11:28–30 (MSG). Jesus called out,

> Are you tired? Worn out? Burned out on religion? Come to me. Get away with me and you'll recover your life. I'll show you how to take a real rest. Walk with me and work with me—watch how I do it. Learn the unforced rhythms of grace. I won't lay anything heavy or ill-fitting on you. Keep company with me and you'll learn to live freely and lightly.

Jesus Christ invites us to join God in the River of grace for the sake of the world. It's the flow of real rest, true freedom, and recovering our lives as well as the life of the world. It is pure gift, but it is not passive. And it doesn't happen primarily between our ears.

Notice all the action words in Jesus's invitation: *come, get away, walk, work, watch, learn, keep company, live.* The invitation is participation. God is already working in every corner of the earth and in every molecule of our lives. As we follow Christ, we get to participate in that eternally flowing good work through practices that allow God's Spirit to do what only God can do. Grace alone makes the River flow, but we need to wade into the water. Grace alone makes the vine grow, but we need to build the trellis. Grace alone makes the wind blow, but spiritual practices help us humbly open the window, day by day, moment by moment. The invitation is participation.

While this invitation requires the complete laying down of our lives as bold and humble living sacrifices, we don't have to do it alone. In fact, we can't do it alone. Answering Jesus's invitation involves a community of swimmers.

Thankfully, you and I are part of a diverse global community that spans thousands of years. The countless women and men who have been swimming in the River have developed invaluable swimming wisdom. One of the greatest gifts of being a Christian is learning from those who swim differently than we do.

I grew up in a Christian system that assumed our version of the tradition possessed all the truth. All others had none of the truth. We guarded what we had and defended our beliefs and decided we couldn't learn from anyone outside our inner circle. But I have found that while my original tradition is committed to and hungry for the truth, it comprises only a thin slice of a much bigger and more fully Christian story. Much of this book will explore what we can learn from Jesus followers who are outside our inner circles.

In addition to learning from others, we have the eternal

Christ swimming with us. We are never alone. Christ keeps calling out, "Come to *me*. . . . Work with *me*. . . . Keep company with *me* . . ." (Matthew 11:28–29, MSG, emphasis added). The Teacher of life does not stand aloof from our search but rather invites us to swim *with him*. The River is a place not of self-actualization but of relationship. We can't fix ourselves to please God, but we can join Christ and get swept up in God's good pleasure to heal the world and us. The invitation is participation.

Will you say yes? Will you move beyond correct belief about the River and jump into the Current with Christ to learn to swim? There are no teachers, traditions, or resources that can help you as long as you choose to remain on the shore.

You and I don't need more ideas or complex philosophies. We need to put the ideas we have already learned into practice. We need to get into the River. Let us wade in with Christ, learn to swim with God's Eternal Current in each moment, and be transformed for the sake of our lives and the sake of the world.

This is a practice-based faith. And we're all invited.

1

Losing My Religion and Finding the Kingdom

On an otherwise-normal Sunday morning in 2002, as I prepared to lead worship at my church, it dawned on me that I didn't believe the words of most of the songs we'd be singing. In fact, even though I was a full-time employee of a large evangelical church in the Chicago suburbs, I was pretty sure I didn't believe in Christianity anymore. Somewhere along the line, between being saved in elementary school and joining the staff at a church, my faith had stopped working. Like a car with a seized engine or an air conditioner that blows only warm air, my life as a Christian had run its course. An observer might see all the right pieces there, but something was uncomfortably absent.

For years I thought Christianity was fundamentally about three things: believing the correct things about God, saying a magic prayer to obtain eternal security, and not doing any of the fun things your friends are doing. It felt like growing up in a small pond that was perfectly safe for beginning swimmers. But once you grew a bit, you began stubbing your toes in the shallows and dreaming about oceans.

I was raised in the Plymouth Brethren faith tradition, a "conservative, low church, nonconformist, evangelical Christian movement whose history can be traced to Dublin, Ireland, in the late 1820s."[1] I experienced it, like any tradition, as a beautiful and messy mixed bag of gifts and disappointments that shaped me deeply. But my overarching reflection is that our church failed to recognize that we were connected to the River of God's kingdom. Instead, we thought we were the one true pond.

This pond was a beautiful place to begin a faith journey. But as I became aware of the larger church and larger world, I started bumping into other realities and versions of the story that didn't fit neatly into our still waters. I was exposed to different ways that Christians throughout history approached Scripture. I encountered a more Charismatic understanding of the Holy Spirit. I discovered that God was not an American— and not even a Republican. I learned that faith and science were not opposites. I got to know Catholics and was scandalized to discover that they, too, were Christians.

This was an exciting yet destabilizing season. I was thrown

off balance because my early Christian training convinced me that anything outside our small pond of Plymouth Brethren beliefs and traditions was wrong. We were the center, and everything else was judged as off center. Instead of teaching us to be curious, they taught us to critique. Instead of teaching us to learn from other people of faith, they taught us to protect ourselves from being led astray. Instead of helping us discern and sift the wheat from the chaff, they trained us to defend ourselves against *anything* that fell outside our circle.

I wish my early tradition would have seen my search and said, "Yes! Keep exploring! Go! We've given you a foundation. Now let it sweep you into the bigger River. Keep growing and learning and building." Instead, church leaders inadvertently communicated, *Nope. We are right; they are wrong. We are inside and have all the rightness; they are outside with none of the rightness. Stay with us or fall away from the faith.*

So for the first twenty-five years of my life, I stayed in the small pond. I wanted to be a good Christian. I loved the people in this faith community, and they loved me. But eventually, from the inside out, my faith began to crumble. And I found myself at the crossroads that so many other people have stood at: Should I double down on a faith that no longer works or abandon the whole thing?

Maybe you have asked this question. Maybe you're asking it right now. Your pond may feel very different from mine, but the ache for more is universal. No matter how good and whole your experience has been, the River is deeper. The Current is stronger. And you were made to get swept up into the fullness of its flowing goodness. Could this be your moment?

Increasingly in this polarized time it can feel as if we have only two choices: give in or give up. We can turn off our hearts to stay where we are, or we can break our hearts by walking away from faith entirely. Friends, these are terrible choices. And thankfully, they are not the only options. But I know first-hand the claustrophobic pain of not being able to identify a third way.

So there I was in my midtwenties on a Sunday morning. I was standing backstage at my church, filled with dread as I prepared to put on a fake Christian smile and rock the house once again. Let me state the obvious: it's pretty awkward to urge people to join you in singing songs you no longer believe.

This season of losing faith was dark. I didn't feel angry as much as sad—and profoundly lost. Very quickly I slipped into a numb sort of despair.

Most often, the despair came out sideways. My disillusion-ment with faith spread to a disillusionment with just about everything and everyone else. Rather than grappling with the terror of feeling the ground disintegrating beneath my feet, I mostly just poked holes in everything else. Everyone was stupid. Everyone was fake. Everything was a lie. This was essentially a matter of self-protection. If I could remain focused on how everyone was wrong, then I wouldn't have to wrestle with the terrifying reality of my own wrongness. But in quiet moments, the unwelcome cries of my disintegrating faith sneaked through my cynic's armor, and in those undefended moments, I felt truly lost.

The Christian story was the wallpaper on nearly every room of my memory—framing every day of my life. I didn't know how to move forward constructively without it.

I'm not the only person who has felt that *giving in* or *giving up* were his or her only options. I needed to find a third way, and I have a hunch that if you're with me this far, you're looking for a third way as well. Jesus called it the narrow road that leads to life (see Matthew 7:14).

You will never settle for a small version of the story, but you're not willing to give up altogether. Thank God. Or maybe you have found a third way and are looking to move more deeply into these streams. In either case, it's possible to take a new path. But it's very difficult to walk the path alone.

A New Way Forward

Thankfully, my parents and a few close friends weren't afraid of the doubts and questions of my midtwenties. In fact, a few of them moved closer to me in my dark season. (This is not normal. Many people express their doubts, only to get kicked out of the community. I am profoundly grateful for such a loving family and for safe, patient, and wise friends.)

A friend named Chris—a musician in my band who would go on to become a brilliant theologian—gave me a life-altering book. Possibly without realizing it, he was saying, *You've been trapped in one small pond for a long time, and you're drowning. But there's a bigger and better River out there! Here's an invitation into an entirely new way of being.* Chris handed me a copy of *The Divine Conspiracy* by Dallas Willard.

I remember the morning I read chapter 2, "Gospels of Sin Management." I was sitting on a fake-wood floor, leaning against a fake-leather couch, when God used Willard's writing to open my eyes to a reality that I had never before heard: the kingdom of God. I learned that Jesus was inviting us not primarily into correct beliefs, an eternal destination, or behavior modification but rather into participation in a living, eternally present reality. Through Christ, we get to join the redemption and restoration of all things. God has not given up on the world. Instead, God invites every one of us—in the way of Jesus and through the power of the Spirit—into the divine conspiracy of overcoming evil with good.

Although I had been a Christian most of my life, this was the first time I had heard teaching on the subject that Jesus devoted most of *his* teaching to. Jesus's primary message in the Gospels is the kingdom of God, but for some reason my tradition had avoided the topic entirely. How could we have missed Jesus's core message?

At first I felt regret and frustration, but these quickly melted into gratitude for the possibility of a new way forward. This was such good news!

As my heart pounded and my vision blurred with tears, I sat on the floor where I had been reading and prayed over and over, "God, if this is what you are up to in the world, I'm in. If this is who you are and what you care about, I'm in. God, if you can use someone like me, in all my doubt and brokenness, I'm in."

And like a good evangelical, I was born again . . . again.

LEARNING TO SWIM

The first few months after being awakened to God's kingdom were full of passion, gratitude, and almost-nuclear energy. Like discovering a treasure buried in my backyard, I had found what was missing, and I threw my whole self into trying to live it out. But while the conversion exuberance carried me for a while, I began to notice that my old tools were no longer fit for this new journey. The skills I relied on to swim in the still pond didn't help me in the raging River. The old wineskins were never meant to hold new wine.

I had finally been drawn into the great Eternal Current that has been flowing throughout history, and I wholeheartedly said yes to Christ's invitation to get into the water. But I didn't know how to swim. I didn't know what to do on Sundays or in my life. My mind had been converted, and my heart was burning with devotion, but I didn't know how to live into it.

So I began exploring.

The years following my spiritual awakening were both glorious and tumultuous, exciting and disillusioning, heart expanding and heartbreaking. The search led me more deeply into myself, and it nudged me outward into corners of the Christian faith that previously would have felt dangerously off limits. My heart had been seized by the mighty River of grace that is good news to all people, and I was going to either learn how to swim with Christ or drown trying.

WORSHIP BEYOND SINGING

This search led my wife, Shauna, and me to Michigan, where we joined with a young pastor named Rob Bell at his church, Mars Hill Bible Church. Our years at Mars Hill were some of the most exciting and stretching of my whole life. It was a greenhouse for artistic experimentation, theological exploration, and discovering what the kingdom of God could look like in an actual time and place. We read books that blew our minds, heard sermons that ignited our hearts, and walked closely with a small group of Jesus followers who will forever frame the way we think about community.

As a worship leader, I tried to align the Mars Hill community with the bigger story, but I quickly discovered that my normal approach was woefully inadequate. Four rock songs and a hymn fell far short of the depth and width of the kingdom vision that animated us. It was like trying to paint Van Gogh's *The Starry Night* masterpiece using only two colors. And so we began to experiment with different forms, practices, and ways to worship. Fortunately, my ministry partner, Troy Hatfield, had been on this journey for many years. He had a huge influence on all that we learned and discovered.

In the same way that God expanded our corporate worship forms to embrace the bigger story, God did the same thing in my soul. Four rock songs and a hymn no longer cut it on Sundays, and my personal spiritual practice began to fall short as well. It was in this season that I heard about contemplative Christianity, and I practiced centering prayer for the first time. I learned about the Jewish roots of our faith and began to see the Scriptures in a new and more vibrant light. Rob Bell's teaching also exposed me to the deep connection between spiritual health and emotional health, and we explored practices that helped us become not just better Christians but, through grace, better humans.

As my internal world was being reshaped and reformed, I learned that God was inviting me outward into the bigger world that God was reshaping and reforming. I didn't always live it out well, but this season was the first time I saw contemplation and activism come together in one community. The deeper we went inside ourselves, the more we felt propelled into the messiness of the world. We didn't have to choose between being isolated contemplatives and being exhausted activists.

Instead, we caught a vision for swimming with Christ in a life of contemplative activism. I will always be grateful for Rob and the Mars Hill family.

In those formative years, both as individuals and as part of a church community, Shauna and I discovered that God's Eternal Current is deeper and grander and more beautifully powerful than we knew. This understanding brought us face to face with our inability to swim well in it. Four songs and a hymn in worship could get our feet wet, but we had to move beyond singing if we were to enter the flow and swim. My personal practice of reading the Bible and journaling was a helpful foundation, but it could take me only so far. Thankfully, God's grace drenched us as we stumbled and splashed around with new (old) practices and worship forms. I couldn't wait to see what was around the corner.

A New Liturgy

In January 2009, after months of conversation and just shy of a billion HR interviews, I accepted a worship leader job back at Willow Creek Community Church. The pastoral team was breathing new life into the weekend services, and they invited me to join the adventure.

Shauna and I had felt it was time to leave Mars Hill, so here we were back in the Chicago suburbs. I jumped into my new role at Willow Creek like an excited kid with a new backpack and school shoes, ready to keep building on the themes we'd explored at Mars Hill. I came to meetings with idea after idea about "swimming in the River" and "moving beyond singing" and pushing and stretching and experimenting and widening the bounds of worship. I was like an overcaffeinated soapbox preacher, relentlessly pushing the church toward an exciting and risky future.

The only thing I didn't do, unfortunately, was listen. I rarely stopped to ask, *What does the team think?* or *How do we build on the beautiful foundation of what has already been laid?* or *Is it possible that I have as much to learn as I have to teach?* Instead, I put my head down and pushed and pushed and pushed.

This was a very difficult season, and I created a lot of heartache—for both everyone around me and myself. I believed so deeply in what a church could be and how we could empower the church to swim with Christ for the sake of the world, but I wasn't mature enough to bring meaningful change.

After a particularly frustrating day of work, I went for a run on the trail that ran through the woods behind my house. The goal was to pray and seek peace, but instead, I became more stressed, more angry, and more tangled up in fear. I had once again fallen into the prayer of rehearsing my anxieties rather than releasing them to God. So I opened iTunes on my phone to find spiritual help. The intent was good, but all the worship music that I found was happy, triumphant, and (in that moment) offensively irrelevant to the reality of my life.

I thought, *I don't need a pep rally. I need to be pastored.*

This burning need sparked an idea. Over the next six months, a few artist friends and I began dreaming, experimenting, and finally producing a series of twenty-five-minute audio recordings called *A New Liturgy.* Through songs, readings, Scripture, and guided prayers, we sought to help people create holy space wherever they find themselves.

The River of God is always flowing—every day and not just on Sundays, in every place and not just in church buildings—and we can learn to swim in each moment. Our cars can become rolling sanctuaries. Our living rooms can become tabernacles. Thanks to God's gracious presence, simple tools, liturgies, and practices can open us up to what God has been doing all along.

In the midst of this difficult and beautiful season of inner turmoil, exciting realizations, and God's gracious healing, while working on *A New Liturgy,* I stumbled into a conversation with Bill Hybels, the senior pastor of our church and who is also my father-in-law. As we discussed the new passions growing in me and how I hoped to bring them more fully into Willow Creek, he said, "Aaron, just so you know, we're never going to do the kinds of liturgies and spiritual practices you want to do in our weekend services. That is not what our services are for."

As he paused, my inner monologue sprinted through the entire cycle of surprise, despair, anger, gratitude, and delight.

He named reality with gracious but shocking clarity, and I was reeling a bit. Then he continued in an unexpected direction: "But you're onto something important."

Record scratch. Wait . . . huh? That wasn't what I expected him to say. It got more surprising:

> Aaron, would you consider pulling together a team to create a space at Willow for people to explore these spiritual practices? We know that we can do more to help Christ-centered people go deep, and I think this could be a huge gift to our community.

This conversation changed the trajectory of my life. Rather than trying to force a square peg into a round hole every Sunday morning, the church was empowering a team and me to create a holy community of unapologetic squares.

I jumped in with both feet. I prayed more than I had ever prayed before. I contacted every like-minded person who was willing to help me learn and discern the right questions. I met with anyone who would teach and inspire the new team I was building. I read every book on spiritual formation and practice-based faith I could get my hands on. I had countless coffee conversations with people who felt the same ache and might want to join the adventure.

Along the way, influenced by experts and fellow journeyers alike and through the grace and wisdom of God's Spirit, we sketched out a proposal for a practice-based, discipleship-focused, neo-liturgical, ecumenical, Eucharistic gathering to take place Sunday nights at Willow Creek. The church leadership approved eighteen months of funding to launch the experiment. We called it the Practice: Learning the Unforced Rhythms of Grace.

Have you ever felt stuck in the shallows and unable to find a new way? Have you ever longed for depths that terrified you yet felt utterly necessary? Have you ever believed your faith was dying, only to find that the death you'd been avoiding was the one possible path to new life?

You're not alone, and you're not crazy. No two journeys are alike, but I share my story in the hope that it will resonate with and encourage you. As we walk together through these pages, may God reawaken the deep longing that always has scratched around in your soul. The Eternal Current is flowing in you right now. By God's grace, it has always been flowing. Let's keep swimming together.

2

The Birth of the Practice

From the beginning, our new, largely experimental community of faith set out to become people who didn't just believe things about Jesus but who would learn to rearrange our lives to put Jesus's words into practice for the sake of the world. We wanted to be not simply hearers but doers as well. Not just students of the River but full-on swimmers.

As our team[1] explored what the Practice should become, we started with a central insight inspired by a team member, Mindy Caliguire: *we can't add spiritual formation to an already overly busy Christian life.* Or, drawing from Mindy's imagery, a person can't drink jet fuel all week and try to light a candle on Sunday nights. That's not how a human soul works.

Christ does not invite us to simply spiritualize how we're already living. Baptizing the American Dream does not make it Christian. As far as we can tell, Christ calls us to finally and completely let go of our self-building projects and get swept up in the River of God's humanity-building project. This vision for a new way to be human begins in us as we humbly rearrange our lives to align with God's restoration from the inside out.

In other words, there is an Eternal Current flowing toward the redemption and restoration of all things, and we've been invited to swim along for the sake of our own lives and the whole world. Fortunately, Christ is a present and gracious teacher, constantly calling out to each one of us,

> Are you tired? Worn out? Burned out on religion? Come to me. Get away with me and you'll recover your life. I'll show you how to take a real rest. Walk with me and work with me—watch how I do it. Learn the unforced rhythms of grace. (Matthew 11:28–29, MSG)

This version of Jesus's words ignited something in our community. Could God's invitation possibly be *this* good? Might we be able to discover its meaning together? Learning the "unforced rhythms of grace" became the anchor point and goal of every conversation, dream, liturgy, teaching, and plan.

WHAT THIS LOOKS LIKE IN PRACTICE

The Practice meets most Sunday nights in the chapel of Willow Creek Community Church. Up until a few years ago, it still had pews with kneelers. The technology in the room is limited, and every part of the room feels like classic church space. It's not cool or edgy, and we love it. For us, it is a perfect space to learn how to put Jesus's words into practice.

When you walk into the chapel for a Practice gathering, the first thing you notice is that the communion table is at the center of the room, with chairs set up in the round, facing the table. This is intentional. Jesus Christ is the center of everything we do, and the Eucharist is the center of everything we practice. The room itself preaches this. We don't have a stage, so whoever is leading, teaching, or talking is at least partially obscured by the bread, juice, and cross at the center.

Further, no matter where you sit, you are looking at the faces of the other half of the community. This is beautiful, unnerving, and intimate. A friend commented after a worship gathering, "At many churches, I can show up and hide. It doesn't cost me anything to attend. But at the Practice, there is nowhere to hide and it forces me to engage. I'm not sure I always like it, but I know I need it."

We want our worship space to feel like a holy living room. Simple, reverent, and human. We long to become a community together, and the Eucharist table is placed in the center because we know that Christ is the center of everything. We believe the room preaches more loudly than any words.

As a worship leader for the last twenty-five years, I find this room setup extremely freeing. And it helps me realize how difficult it can be to lead worship in an elevated, stage-centric context. When worshippers find they are looking up at a person onstage, it makes that person the central figure in the room, from a visual standpoint. If the room is set up to focus every eye on the worship leader or speaker, what else could we be expected to think? Most worship leaders sincerely want to point people to God, but the stages they stand on can get in the way.

Physical space is not neutral. The room itself preaches. The container shapes everything we place inside it, for good or for bad. It became clear to us that all these decisions really matter.

WORSHIP IN RHYTHMS OF UNFORCED GRACE

Each gathering is broken into three parts: (1) an opening liturgy, (2) a teaching that leads into practice, and (3) the Eucharist, which sends us out into the world. Some nights the three parts are closely tied together thematically. Other nights they aren't. But they always flow together as a single journey.

We gather to learn to see where God's Current is flowing in our lives and in the world, to explore and practice swimming patterns that help us swim with Christ in the River, and to get launched by the Spirit into the River of God's kingdom for the sake of our lives and the life of the world.

To do this, we anchored the Practice experiment in six values. I've come to believe that, broadly speaking, they are indispensable guideposts for every individual and community that wants to swim in the Eternal Current. They are not the only values, and I'm wary to even imply a one-size-fits-all solution, but I can personally attest to the powerful ways that these six values help keep us in the Current.

1. Staying Centered on the Kingdom Keeps Us in the Current

Jesus has invited us to join God in healing and redeeming the world. Through the Scriptures, story, and worship, we want to align ourselves with this good work.

Without a big-picture kingdom vision, spiritual practices can be weird and unhelpful. They can become a way to try to earn God's blessing and establish spiritual superiority or to avoid reality as we hide in prayer closets. Separated from the big story of God's kingdom, spiritual practices (or anything we do) can become mere religious tools that often help us miss the point.

We can't allow the practices to become the point. Author and innovative thinker Simon Sinek wrote a helpful book titled *Start with Why*. He shows the importance of asking *why* before one asks *how* or *what* in any endeavor.[2] Our *why* of swimming with the Eternal Current is to align with the kingdom of God. Our *how* is through spiritual practices. Our *what* is a community of practice.

Or to use the River metaphor, our *why* is that we want to

get swept up in God's River of restoration. Our *how* is that we join Christ in the water to learn to swim with the Current. Our *what* is that we are a community committed to swimming together.

At the Practice, nearly every gathering involves hearing the big story again. We use the first few minutes to offer a kingdom context for the spiritual practice we will focus on that evening. These practices include breath prayer, the Examen, praying for the world through images, Lectio Divina, centering prayer, lament, and many other historic and modern practices. But we always begin with a reminder of the big kingdom story.

2. A Practice-Based Approach
Keeps Us in the Current

To learn how to swim with Christ requires church gatherings to be more like a gymnasium than a classroom. We don't need just to learn the facts; we need to focus on the activities that help us live out the facts and join Christ in the water.

If information alone could transform us into Christlikeness, then we would be the most Christlike generation of all time. We have unlimited access to all the knowledge in human history through the smartphones in our pockets, yet the world doesn't seem to be moving quickly toward a holy utopia. Why is this?

Philosopher James K. A. Smith, in his game-changing book

Desiring the Kingdom, suggests that humans are not fundamentally thinking beings. We're not even primarily believing beings, but at our core, he wrote, we are "defined fundamentally by love."[3] So schools, teachers, and churches that try to change people by giving them information fail to address the core issue: we become what we love. The path of change involves redirecting our love toward a different object, not filling our heads with ideas. This redirection primarily happens through participating in certain formative practices.

Rather than approaching our church gatherings as a classroom (to fill our minds with information) or a concert hall (to move our hearts with emotion), we long to create a spiritual gymnasium, which can form our whole selves. Our minds and hearts are critical parts of ourselves but not enough on their own. It's important to know what Jesus taught and to desire to obey, but we also need a place to learn the practices that will rearrange our lives. Only then can we become holistic people who can live out Jesus's teachings in our everyday living.

Simply believing about the River is not enough. Singing passionate River songs is helpful but not enough. Jesus has invited us, through spiritual practice, to wade into the water and allow God to do—in us and through us—what only God can do. We all need a community of fellow swimmers learning to bring every part of our lives into the center of the Current with Christ.

3. Empowering Beyond Sunday
Keeps Us in the Current

According to Ephesians 4, the church exists to equip the people for ministry (see verses 11–12). A Sunday service is not the main event but rather a training ground to help all of us become people who can live the way Jesus would if he were in our place.[4]

I can never get over the beauty of the priesthood of all believers. Through Christ, we all have equal access to God, and through the Spirit, we all can be ministers of the good news. I believe this theological concept reminds us that the church is not just a top-down institution but rather a body of empowered image bearers of our Creator.

For instance, please allow me to oversimplify a bit for the sake of contrast. (Most churches don't fall fully into either extreme.) In a church *for* the people—a church focused exclusively on what the leadership can do for those who occupy the pews—worship means "Come hear our gifted artists provide a worship experience that will inspire and bless you. When it's done, you'll want to give them a round of applause and be glad you attended."

But in a church *of* the people, worship becomes prayerful, intentional space that empowers the people to cocreate a worship experience both as individuals and as a body, both when we are home and when we are together. The church helps people connect with God and one another—and then gets out of the people's way.

In a church *for* the people, evangelism means "Bring your friend to church to hear the pastor preach the gospel." This type of church entrusts the kingdom-of-God message to experts and often reduces the sweeping story of God to disembodied information that people are encouraged to believe but not always to practice.

In contrast, a church *of* the people practices evangelism by training disciples and launching them to serve the world and share their stories. Such an approach helps foster a community so alive and beautiful that people are eager to participate.

In a church *for* the people, mission means "Give your money to the church so it can carry out a ministry to the poor." Attendees simply write checks and the church will make sure things get taken care of.

But a church *of* the people declares, "No one knows the poor in your town better than you. Let us help you serve them. And if you don't know the poor in your town, following Jesus means that you'll need to make some changes. Please let us help you learn from and serve the poor."

Inspired by the teaching of Ephesians 4 and the priesthood of all believers, a church of the people declares, "You can do it! If the Spirit of God is inside you and you are connected to your sisters and brothers in Christ, then you can be the hands and feet of God in the world." A church of the people is a Spirit-empowered training community that is more about launching than retaining, more about empowering than directing. And at its best, a church of the people sounds a lot like the Home Depot's old slogan: "You can do it. We can help."

4. Ecumenical Humility Keeps Us in the Current

Since the Eternal Current is wider than any one Christian tradition, we are blessed by humbly learning from other Christian traditions and practices. As an evangelical for most of my life, I believe evangelicalism is full of truth and can be helpful to the world. But it's only a small segment of the church universal. When we see it as one chapter in the diverse, eternal, global story of God's kingdom on earth, our eyes are opened to so much more of who God is and how we can participate.

We need the beautiful diversity of the body of Christ (see 1 Corinthians 12:15–27). We must recapture our ability to learn from those outside our circle. Conviction is a beautiful thing, but so is humility. We long to be people who admit what we don't know and then humbly partner with those who can teach us.

At the Practice we declare, "Jesus is the center and focus of everything we do, but we acknowledge our limited vantage point. We embrace and learn from any tradition or practice that elevates Christ and forms us into his likeness." Reading ancient prayers? Yes. Singing pop songs with our hands in the air? Yes. Passing the Peace? Yes. Singing old spiritual laments? Yes.

Just as each member of a church is one part of the body, I wonder if each church tradition needs to be understood as one part of the bigger body of Christ. Each is absolutely critical, but each on its own is only one part of the story. Fundamentalist Christians remind us that God's truth is profoundly important. Catholic Christians remind us that we are called to work for good in the world. Evangelical Christians remind us that we need to be saved. Episcopalian and Anglican Christians remind us to keep our hearts and minds open to all the things God is doing on earth, even things that might surprise us.

Each one is a glorious part of the tangible kingdom of God among us. And how can the "eye . . . say to the hand, 'I don't need you!'" (1 Corinthians 12:21)?

Over the last few years, those who assemble as the Practice have learned from a Jesuit priest, a self-described progressive Pentecostal hillbilly preacher, an Anglican canon theologian, an Eastern Orthodox teacher, a rabbi, an Episcopal priest, a number of justice workers and peacemakers, an Emergent leader, and a feminist Christian, as well as medical doctors, therapists, pastors, artists . . . and even evangelical Christians. These brilliant women and men have stretched us to see how wide, deep, long, and high is the love of God through Christ and to see the expansive beauty of the diverse ways to swim.

5. The Eucharist Keeps Us in the Current

The weekly practice of communion anchors us in Christ's death, resurrection, and promise of return.

My good friend and mentor Rory Noland remarked, "You know, Aaron, for most of church history, the pastor's lecture was not the central part of the service." I was surprised, to say the least. Up to that point, I was familiar with only the evangelical order of worship: worship music, announcements, and a forty-five-minute sermon. Or in the worst case: warm-up songs, offering, and the Main Event.

Rory had been studying church history. He pointed out that over the last two thousand years the church had commonly seen the Eucharist as the high point of any gathering. The sermon was important, but mostly to prepare people to meet Christ at the table. The Eucharist was the focus, and every part of the service led to this holy moment.

The more I explored a Eucharistic theology, the more it came alive in ways I had never imagined. It began spilling into how I saw all of life. Reading *For the Life of the World* by Orthodox priest and theologian Alexander Schmemann unlocked a sacramental door in my heart that keeps opening wider. (I need to reread this book once a year, forever.) But reading about the Eucharist isn't enough. The weekly practice of celebrating the Eucharist is changing my life and transforming our community.

The Practice's worship space, which I've mentioned is set up in the round, says *Christ is at the center.* Everything revolves around the bread and juice, and every gathering builds to this point, helping us begin to live into one of the mysteries of our faith:

> Communion is participation with a presence, not merely remembrance. The bread and wine don't simply help us look back at what Jesus did; they help us get swept up in what Christ is doing now, today, every moment in every place on earth.[5]

Many volumes have been written about the deep mystery and centrality of the Eucharist, based on lifetimes of studying and practicing. I am clearly not one of those writers and will not attempt to explain what I am only beginning to understand. I will, however, testify to what I've experienced. A weekly practice of holy communion is re-forming me from the inside out.

Before we come to the table each week, we pray through a liturgy, based largely on the Anglican Eucharistic liturgy. (This has been incredibly important to those of us who grew up in nonliturgical traditions.) Each Sunday as we approach the table, we are reminded of and included in the huge story that God is writing in human history. The story centers on the redemptive arc of creation, fall, redemption, and restoration. And by amazing grace, we are invited to participate in this eternal and constantly unfolding story.

No matter the text we're studying, the topic we're exploring, or the practice we're participating in, every gathering guides us to engage the living presence of Christ at the communion table. Where else would we turn?

6. Community Keeps Us in the Current

The Christian life is not meant to be practiced alone. A life of faith is a communal journey. If we are merely a group of individuals on parallel personal journeys, it won't work. It can't. God created us not to be independent, self-contained individuals but rather to be interdependent members of a whole.

At the Practice, we struggled with the best ways to flesh this out in a practice-based gathering. While our convictions about community have only deepened, we spun our wheels for the first few years as we tried to integrate the contemplative inward journey with the communal nature of God's invitation. We found it difficult to create a safe enough space for the intimate work God wanted to do in each person while simultaneously encouraging each person to step out of his or her comfort zone to connect with other people. The energies of the inward and communal journeys seemed consistently to be at odds.

Then in 2017, Pastor Jason Feffer created Practice Tables. This was the wise and simple framework we needed to bring individual stories and practices into safe and holy community. Once a month, the Practice gathers in homes around tables instead of coming together in the chapel. Eight to twelve people meet in a home to share a meal, pray a short liturgy, and offer a part of their stories to one another.

This quickly became a powerful way to support one another on the journey. In Jason's words, "Every one of us has a need to be seen and known. At our tables, we create an environment for Christ's presence to become tangible in the seeing and knowing of loving community."

These six values have kept us in the Eternal Current—both as a practice-based community and as individual Christ followers. The more we submit to and orient our lives around these guideposts, the more they open us to Christ's gracious invitation to swim. I could tell you story after story of how God met our community in this messy and glorious stumble into the River. I wish you could meet the incredible swimmers of the Practice.

This journey is changing my life. Not all at once. Definitely not in ways that I would have predicted or even chosen. But in the midst of the brokenness of the world, the messiness of the modern church, and my propensity to sink more than swim, I've never been more thankful for the way of Christ. I've honestly never been more grateful to be a Christian. Thanks be to God.

Friend, you can join us. And by *us* I mean *the billions of imperfect human beings throughout history who have stumbled into the Eternal Current by grace and learned to swim.* You really can. It will look different for each of us—depending on each person's story, history, and background—but these six values can help keep you in the Current, swept up with Christ for the sake of the world.

In the next few chapters, we'll dig deep to explore how each value can support and propel every one of us to swim with God's River in our lives, churches, neighborhoods, and families. Let us begin with the big story.

3

Swimming with the River

The Kingdom of God

Until you understand the object of the game, it's very difficult to play well. Without knowing the destination of a road trip, you probably won't end up there. And if we are unclear about Jesus's central invitation, we will struggle to follow him. In the spiritual life—as with every area of reality—we must begin with the big story.

For years, I thought the Christian story primarily dealt with my sin problem. I thought of it as a solution I needed so I could go to heaven after I die. The gospel was presented in this form: you're a sinner, Jesus died for your sins, and you need to say a certain prayer to apply his blood to your guilt so you can have eternal life. We called this "the gospel," but it didn't sound like very good news for the actual life I was living here and now.

Over the years, I began to understand that the invitation of Christ has to do with far more than my personal salvation. While I am clearly a sinner and my only hope is Christ, securing a guarantee about my eternal destination did not seem to be Jesus's central concern. It took me a long time to admit I was questioning the core of the story. It felt like betraying my faith. But while God used the smaller version of the story to get me started on a spiritual journey, it eventually ran out of gas. The gospel was never meant to be stripped down to a ticket to heaven.

New Testament theologian N. T. Wright has stated it this way:

> The question of what happens to me after death is *not* the major, central, framing question that centuries of theological tradition have supposed. The New Testament, true to its Old Testament roots, regularly insists that the major, central, framing question is that of God's purpose of rescue and re-creation for the whole world, the entire cosmos. The destiny of individual human beings must be understood within that context.[1]

If the goal is getting our souls into heaven, then every part of the Christian life (except evangelism) is secondary. Discipleship becomes optional. Mission and community become mere add-ons. But the story of God that Jesus embodied goes far beyond a onetime salvation transaction.

Wright added this:

> The whole point of what Jesus was up to was that he was doing, close up, in the present, what he was promising long-term, in the future. And what he was promising for that future, and doing in that present, was not saving souls for a disembodied eternity but rescuing people from the corruption and decay of the way the world presently is so they could enjoy, already in the present, that renewal of creation which is God's ultimate purpose—and so they could thus become colleagues and partners in that larger project.[2]

Can I get an "Amen"? We've been invited to become colleagues and partners with God in the larger project of healing and restoring all things for the sake of the world.

When we begin to grasp the nature of God's invitation and the amazing grace that makes it possible, then every part of our lives matters. We learn to forgive so that bitterness can't hold us back. We cultivate our God-given talents so they can be used to help the whole. We soak in the Scriptures to let God's story wash over us. We draw close to the poor because Christ is with them in a special way. Discipleship and mission and community no longer sound like optional add-ons but are essential to living fully into the invitation. When we get clear about the full extent of the big story, a practice-based life becomes a tangible way to humbly say yes to God.

Wright finished with these words:

> What you *do* in the present—by painting, preaching, singing, sewing, praying, teaching, building hospitals, digging wells, campaigning for justice, writing poems, caring for the needy, loving your neighbor as yourself—*will last into God's future.* These activities are not simply ways of making the present life a little less beastly, a little more bearable, until the day when we leave it behind altogether. . . . They are part of what we may call *building for God's kingdom.*[3]

We have been invited, in the way of Christ and by the power of the Spirit, to build for God's kingdom on earth. A quick word about the phrase *kingdom of God*.

THE LANGUAGE OF KINGDOM

Throughout the book, I will use the phrase that Jesus used in the Scriptures—*kingdom of God* or *kingdom of heaven*—to mean "the realm where God's will happens on earth as it happens in heaven." This can be a physical location, an internal posture, or a social reality, but it always involves some kind of *thin place* where God's dream for humanity breaks into reality like a green shoot reaching up through a crack in the concrete. Jesus Christ invites us to partner with God in this subversively redemptive vision and build a world that makes more space for it to flourish.

That being said, I struggle with how this vision has developed into an overly masculine, top-down understanding of the word *kingdom*. First, God is Spirit, not male or female in the human sense, and our tradition of using primarily masculine language for God has told only half the story. Second, the word *kingdom* can imply a top-down, conquering power, like the kingdoms of this world. It's worth noting that Jesus embodied a life exactly counter to the world's coercive power, and his teachings about God's kingdom were always from the bottom up: a mustard seed, yeast in bread, a buried treasure, a party for the outcasts, and so on.

A helpful substitute for the word *kingdom* can be *realm* or the more relational word *kindom*. Feel free to make one of those substitutes as you read. (I'm just scratching the surface of an enormous topic here. For a brilliant deep dive into the history and theology of the kingdom of God, read Scot McKnight's book *King Jesus Gospel*.)

Anchoring Your Community in God's Story

Learning how to build for God's kingdom requires communal practices as well as personal practices. Let's begin with two ways we anchor the faith community that I'm part of.

First, we talk about it, again and again. For nearly three months in 2015, I began every gathering of the Practice by proclaiming,

> There is a great and mighty River flowing throughout history toward the healing and restoration of all things. Jesus called this the kingdom of God, where what God wants to happen happens. But he didn't say, "Believe about this River." He invited us to join him in it and to learn how to swim with the Current for the sake of the world. Tonight we will learn to swim through the practice of _____.

In that context, our concrete practice (the Examen or centering prayer or confession or another) was always seen as the means to participate in what God is already doing.

Without a kingdom vision, spiritual practices can get pretty weird. Rather than offering unforced rhythms of grace, they can become burdens that weigh us down. Rather than opening

ourselves to God's work in and through us, they can become
ways to enhance our own lives or try to earn God's favor. Rather
than connecting us to God, spiritual practices without a kingdom vision can even become a way to avoid God. Jesus's words
to the Pharisees in Matthew 23 capture this:

> Woe to you, teachers of the law and Pharisees, you
> hypocrites! You give a tenth of your spices—mint, dill
> and cumin. But you have neglected the more important
> matters of the law—justice, mercy and faithfulness. You
> should have practiced the latter, without neglecting the
> former. You blind guides! You strain out a gnat but
> swallow a camel.
>
> Woe to you, teachers of the law and Pharisees, you
> hypocrites! You clean the outside of the cup and dish,
> but inside they are full of greed and self-indulgence.
> Blind Pharisee! First clean the inside of the cup and
> dish, and then the outside also will be clean.
>
> Woe to you, teachers of the law and Pharisees, you
> hypocrites! You are like whitewashed tombs, which look
> beautiful on the outside but on the inside are full of the
> bones of the dead and everything unclean. In the same
> way, on the outside you appear to people as righteous
> but on the inside you are full of hypocrisy and wicked-
> ness. (verses 23–28)

Without a clear view of the big story, it's easy to turn the means into the end and get lost in the religious weeds. We focus on perfecting the *how,* forget to submit to the *why,* and completely miss the *whom.* This path leads to a split reality in which our outsides get more religious but our insides remain unchanged. I've wandered down this path at times, and it's a miserable way to live. Thankfully, Jesus's invitation is sweepingly beautiful, the Holy Spirit's presence is always near, and God's River is unending grace.

Second, our community practices concrete actions that help align us with God's kingdom throughout the week. We begin with vision and learning but never let it stop at mere belief. The goal always is to swim!

In one of Jesus's many teachings about the kingdom, he said,

The kingdom of heaven is like treasure hidden in a field.
When a man found it, he hid it again, and then in his
joy went and sold all he had and bought that field.
(Matthew 13:44)

The man caught a vision of the kingdom and *in his great joy* sold everything to get it. Friends, this is the entire story. The invitation of Christ is so compelling—such truly good news—that seeing it creates great joy. If your faith feels like a heavy burden, then it's not the way of Jesus, who proclaims freedom, sight, favor, faith, hope, and love. Catching a clear vision of the treasure of this grace-soaked kingdom, if only for a moment, will unleash a spring of joy inside us that wants to gush out.

But notice what the spring of joy caused the man in the story to do. He sold everything to get the treasure. Kingdom joy propelled him into constructive action. He wasn't content to just see and believe in the treasure. Instead, he traded his entire life to receive it. This is a kingdom-powered, practice-based life. This is what it means to swim in the Eternal Current. The treasure is pure gift for all who are delighted enough to reorient their lives in order to swim in this new reality.

In the next few chapters, we'll explore tangible ways to joyfully reorient our lives, communities, families, and even churches around this invitation. But the journey must begin with eyes to see what is already true: God's kingdom is wherever God is working, and God is always working *here*.

UNDERSTAND WHERE GOD ALREADY IS

The River flows eternally and we are constantly near it. Wherever we are, God is already there. God is not a localized Being whom we have to convince to move from far to close. God is here. Therefore, I would suggest that swimming with the Eternal Current invites us to retire a number of common phrases from our Christian vocabulary. Let's reconsider using two of them: "And then God showed up" and "God, we invite you here today."

I know phrases such as these are well intentioned. But when we insert "And then God showed up" as we tell our stories, we say something confusing about God. The same is true when we pray, "God, we invite you here." Where do we think God is? If we claim that God "showed up," are we saying that God was absent prior to that moment? If we beg God to "fill this place today" or to "be with us as we drive," are we suggesting that God would be absent otherwise? Where in the world do we think God is?

The Scriptures are clear about God's location.

Where can I go from your Spirit?
    Where can I flee from your presence?
If I go up to the heavens, you are there;
    if I make my bed in the depths, you are there.
        (Psalm 139:7–8)

Saint Paul taught that God "is not far from any one of us. 'For in him we live and move and have our being'" (Acts 17:27–28).

Jesus declared, "Surely I am with you always, to the very end of the age" (Matthew 28:20).

This theme continues throughout the Scriptures and the

history of God's people. Where is God? God is here. Always. Everywhere.

Some scholars believe that a more accurate translation of "Our Father, who art in heaven" is "Our Father, in the heavens." In other words, "Our Father, who already floods this place and fills the atmosphere—every molecule from the farthest solar system to the inside of my lungs." Or in pastor and author John Ortberg's beautiful phrase, "Our Father who is closer than the air I breathe."[4]

Father Richard Rohr has built on this idea in his brilliant book *Everything Belongs.*

> My starting point is that we're already there. We cannot attain the presence of God because we're already totally in the presence of God. What's absent is awareness. Little do we realize that God is maintaining us in existence with every breath we take. As we take another it means that God is choosing us now and now and now.[5]

The invitation on Sunday morning is the same invitation on Monday morning and Tuesday afternoon: to become present to the God who is already fully present to us. Through spiritual practices, loving one another, and profound humility, we can cultivate eyes to see what is already happening. Likewise, our hearts begin to soften and remain increasingly open to the God who always is open to us and everyone else. Or as Jesus said, "Come to me. . . . Work with me. . . . Keep company with me and you'll learn to live freely and lightly" (Matthew 11:28–30, MSG).

The classic book *The Practice of the Presence of God* by Brother Lawrence may be the most important (and simple) book ever written on keeping company with Christ. Brother Lawrence learned to practice the presence of Christ primarily through his work as a dishwasher.

> [Brother Lawrence] thought it was a shame that some people pursued certain activities (which, he noted, they did rather imperfectly due to human shortcomings), mistaking the means for the end. He said that our sanctification does not depend as much on changing our activities as it does on doing them for God rather than for ourselves.[6]

EYES TO SEE GOD'S WORK OF GRACE

If we are already fully submerged in the presence of God and the reality of the kingdom, then every moment becomes an opportunity to open our eyes and partner with God's present work of grace. While putting our kids to bed, we can partner with God's work in our kids, or we can miss out. When we get into a fender bender, we can partner with God's work in the person who wasn't paying attention and hit our car, or we can miss out. When our boss overlooks or mistreats us, we can partner with God's work in and through the situation, or we can miss out. Every moment offers an opportunity to align with God's immersive presence and get swept up in God's healing activities in our lives and the life of the world. Every moment beckons us to swim.

But how do we cultivate eyes to see the Current? How do we become aware of what has been true all along? Jesus ended several of his teachings with the odd and provocative appeal, "Whoever has ears to hear, let them hear" (see, for example, Mark 4:9). Simply being in the presence of the Teacher of life apparently is not enough. Jesus's audience—then and now— needs to cultivate ears to hear and eyes to see in order to receive his words.

A modern-day example: At this moment, hundreds of AM and FM radio waves are passing through our bodies and eardrums, but they are imperceptible to us. It doesn't matter how hard we try to listen or how many new stations are added. We simply don't have ears to hear radio waves. But if we turn on a radio and tune it to the right frequency, we can receive the fullness of the waves that we're already swimming in. Such a mechanistic example doesn't capture the organically relational aspect of life with Christ, but it can remind us that we must cultivate eyes to see and ears to hear what has been true all along. But how?

For the last four years, I've been meeting for spiritual direction with a wise Jesuit priest, Father Michael Sparough. He sits with me for an hour each month and, like all gifted spiritual directors, prayerfully helps me notice the work of God in my life. He often reminds me that "the title 'spiritual director' is a misnomer. The Holy Spirit is the spiritual director, Aaron. All I do is join you in listening to the Spirit's direction." What a gift. God has used Father Michael's gentle presence in many ways to help me notice the Spirit's fingerprints in my life. Especially during tumultuous seasons of pain, heartbreak, or confusion, when my spiritual senses get dulled, God's grace and clarity have flowed through this humble spiritual director.[7]

In addition to sitting with me each month to help me listen to God, Father Michael also teaches a daily practice that is transforming my life from the inside out. It's known as the Examen.

A SPIRITUAL PRACTICE
FROM SAINT IGNATIUS

One of the most powerful ways to learn how to see God's present kingdom is the prayer of Examen. This historic prayer practice helps us notice where God's River has been flowing each day. It also helps us see the ways we swim with it or against it.

T. S. Eliot famously wrote,

We had the experience but missed the meaning,

And approach to the meaning restores the experience

In a different form.[8]

Many of us live in a swirl of motion, and it's easy to let daily activities propel us forward without our ever dipping below the surface to notice what matters most. God constantly plants seeds of life in and around us, but we rarely slow down to notice. The Examen has been the single most life-giving practice for me over the last five years.

Saint Ignatius of Loyola developed the Examen more than four centuries ago. He suggested that each follower of Christ should stop once or twice a day for fifteen minutes and reflect on his or her day in God's presence. Over time this discipline opens our eyes to the holy possibilities of the reality in which we live.

Praying the Examen

Here's a simple version of the prayer in five steps.

1. Invite the Holy Spirit's Guidance

The Examen is not primarily a self-help technique or self-examination process; it is a way to create holy space in which to carry on a holy conversation. The Examen is not about figuring out what God is doing in our lives. Rather, it invites God to show us what God is already doing in our lives. That distinction sets the trajectory and posture for the experience. We begin with this humble prayer from 1 Samuel 3:10: "Speak, for your servant is listening."

2. Review the Day in Thanksgiving

Saint Ignatius taught that we should begin to look back with gratitude. As a melancholy artist, I found this to be a challenge at first. But now it has become the most important part of the Examen for me. Why? Because God's abundance is the foundation of the universe. Scarcity is very real in the moment, but it will not have the last word. And noticing the good blessings in life that point to the ultimate Reality is transformative. "Every good and perfect gift is from above, coming down from the Father of the heavenly lights, who does not change like shifting shadows" (James 1:17). We should never deny the very real heartache and horror of life, but we dare not place them at the center. We anchor every Examen in thanksgiving.

3. Notice the Feelings That Surface

As we review the last hour or day or week in thanksgiving, we begin to notice the feelings that surface—both positive and negative. We don't judge them as good or bad. We simply notice the feelings with humble curiosity. One of Saint Ignatius's key insights is that our emotions often speak truth in ways that our brains have missed or rationalized or avoided. Our feelings are not the entire story, of course, but they often contain a crucial part of the story. We are blessed when we allow them to come to light in God's presence.

4. Pray from These Feelings

As emotions rise, we ask the Spirit to help us choose one or two emotions to pray about. We begin by telling God what we feel—pouring out our hearts to the One who made us. Then we stop and listen. This is where the holiest of spaces can open up. Sometimes God speaks; other times it sounds like silence. I've experienced seismic moments with God during an Examen, and I've also been distracted and bored. God is not an equation to be solved but a relationship to be cultivated. God is love. God made us and is eternally present in our lives, tirelessly working for healing and good. All we can do is make the space to become present to this Presence.

5. Look Forward to Tomorrow in Hope

As we finish our Examen, we turn toward the future. Father Michael suggests that we ask the question "What do I want to hold on to from today that I can be especially conscious of tomorrow?" As we reflect on the pattern of God's grace in our lives, over time we learn new ways to engage the future with this grace. The Examen helps us notice the past so we can learn from it. Often we end this time of prayer by asking God to propel us into the world with a new sense of God's presence, a new depth of wisdom, a renewed faith that God always is with us and for us. At that point, our eyes are a little more open to see.

Every part of this is God's work, of course. We don't generate any of the good fruit by praying the Examen. But we must choose to make space for it. We don't cause the River to flow; it's already flowing for eternity. All we do is get into the water and let the Current carry us where it wants to go.[9]

A Prayer for Each Moment

Monthly spiritual direction can help you learn to notice God's kingdom and fingerprints in your life. In addition, a daily practice of the Examen is a stunningly powerful tool to cultivate eyes to see. But let me end this chapter with a moment-by-moment prayer to help us swim with God's River. I try to pray some form of it before every conversation, interaction, and decision. It has opened up kingdom possibilities in even the most mundane moments.

Loving God,
who fills the universe,
this entire room,
myself, and everyone in it,
please help me notice what you are doing
—in me and in the other person—
and join that good work.

In the context of a kingdom theology, the guidance of a wise spiritual director, and the formation of a daily Examen, this humble prayer changes everything. Would you try it? Next time you are meeting a friend for coffee, pray this prayer as you're walking into the coffee shop. Next time you are hurrying to a meeting at work, whisper this prayer and see what God does. Next time you are driving to pick up your kid and her three loudest friends, pray this prayer and let God turn your car into a rolling sanctuary.

The Eternal Current constantly flows in you, me, and everyone else. All that is missing is awareness. May God grant you eyes to see it, a heart to get into the water, and arms to swim with the River wherever it flows for the sake of your life and the life of the world.

To do this fully, we'll need a place to learn how to swim and practice with fellow swimmers. Toward that end, let's explore what a practice-based gathering can look like.

Church as a Gymnasium (Part 1)

A Practice-Based Faith

Once upon a time there was a woman who decided to train for a triathlon. After years of struggling with her health and self-image, she gathered the courage to drive to the local fitness center to get some help. The fitness staff greeted her warmly and invited her into a lecture hall. For about ninety minutes, a U2 cover band performed, and then a charismatic personal trainer gave an inspiring talk about fitness.

The woman left encouraged and couldn't wait to go back. Over the next couple of months, she attended this lecture every week and learned a lot about health. The problem is she didn't get in shape. Why? Because no one invited her to the workout floor. She gained a mind full of great information but no skills or practices to bring the knowledge to bear on her body. Her thoughts about running changed, but the legs that would need to do the running remained exactly the same.

The modern church has much in common with this fitness center. We often are good at teaching, talking, and helping people learn important truths. But we rarely give them the tools or training to live out those truths. Preaching is a great first step but a terrible entire plan. Church as classroom is not enough. And beyond teaching, we often excel at offering worship music and inspiring art that move people's hearts. But inspiration without spiritual formation doesn't bring lasting change. Church as concert hall is not enough.

If the people who run the fitness center in our story wanted to help the woman get ready for the race, they would need to rethink their approach. Instead of limiting their input to music and lectures, a personal trainer would get to know the woman, learn about her history and dreams for the future, and formulate a training plan. Then, a couple of times every week, the trainer would meet the woman on the exercise floor to help her take consistent steps toward her goal. This would involve some teaching but always in the context of practice, encouragement, challenge, and the community of fellow fitness center members.

This is, of course, what a local fitness center does. It also seems to have been Jesus's primary approach with his disciples. Still, the modern approach to church often falls far short.

FORMATION, NOT INFORMATION

TED Talks exist to share mind-blowing information, and Broadway shows exist to create heart-expanding art, but only the church exists to form us into Christlikeness for the sake of the world. Correct information and compelling art are important in the church but primarily to help us participate in the human and divine work of spiritual formation. What does this mean?

In his book *Invitation to a Journey,* New Testament professor Dr. M. Robert Mulholland Jr. defined spiritual formation as "the process of being conformed to the image of Christ for the sake of others."[1] We humbly arrange our lives to spend the most possible time in the flow of what God is trying to do inside us. Over time, through divine grace and our imperfect but humble participation in this work, we are transformed into people who naturally think and act as Jesus Christ would if in our place. The invitation into spiritual formation is seen throughout the Scriptures and church history.[2]

But as James K. A. Smith stated, learning about something is not enough. We change only when the object of our love changes.[3] We change when our hearts change. Information alone doesn't transform people; we need practices that shape our desires. And this is why liturgy—both liturgies of the church and liturgies of everyday life—is so powerful.

On Sunday nights at the faith community I'm part of, we

begin with an opening liturgy that helps slow us down, connect us to God's Spirit and to one another, and form us into Christ-likeness through the brilliance of historic liturgical practices. A number of elements are included each night, and my friend and teacher Dr. John Witvliet did much to help shape the approach we take. John is director of the Calvin Institute of Christian Worship and a professor at Calvin College and Calvin Theological Seminary in Grand Rapids, Michigan.

He taught two lessons that have shaped our gatherings. First, he shared a simple image.

> When a child is about a year old, they enter that difficult preverbal stage of grunts and gibberish, and the kindest thing a parent can do is give them language to express what is going on inside of them. We teach them words like "I'm hungry" and "I'm scared" and "I want that ball." This is a huge gift to them. (And us!) But at a certain point, good parents need to also teach their kids language that the children would never choose to say but will form them into the kind of adults we know they need to become. Words like "Thank you" and "I'm sorry" and "Please." This language—that they would never naturally express without us—forms them through repetition into people they might not otherwise become.
>
> Helping your kids express themselves is a needed

and wonderful gift, but the higher role of a parent is
to help form them into whole and healthy adults.[4]

As John finished sharing this image, my head pretty much exploded. For fifteen years as a worship leader, I had focused exclusively on helping people express themselves to God. I sought new ways to help Christians articulate what was most authentic in their hearts, and I offered them songs and prayers to express that truth with sincerity. This form of *expressive worship* is necessary and important; it is a gift to many people. But it's only half the story.

At a certain point in the journey, if we want to grow up into the fullness of Christ (see Ephesians 4:13), we must also participate in *formative worship*. Grounded in the goodness of expressing our authentic hearts to God, we also submit to songs, prayers, and practices that we would never naturally say but that can form us into the Christ followers we long to become.

Consider this example. For a highly activistic, outward-oriented church, an important and formative practice could be to create space in each service to "be still, and know" that God is God (Psalm 46:10) and to practice listening to God's still, small voice. This doesn't always come naturally for action-oriented communities, but it could be powerfully helpful as the people mature into contemplative activists.

Or if a church is great at prayer and the inward journey but tends to get disconnected from God's heart for the outside world, one formative practice might be to create space in each service to pray specifically for the world and to practice saying, "Here am I. Send me!" (Isaiah 6:8). This won't always feel natural, but it could help form the contemplative folks into more activistic contemplatives.

In 2016, as the most contentious US presidential election cycle in recent history was under way, we instituted a formative practice in our opening liturgy. Every Sunday night, following the confession and assurance, we practiced Jesus's teaching to pray for our enemies. Sometimes this would be a global or national enemy (a foreign dictator, either major party's presidential nominee), and sometimes it would be very personal for each attendee (someone who had hurt that person and had become like an enemy). Often we'd pray for both types of enemies. Although this form of prayer doesn't come naturally to most of us, we knew it would be profoundly forming over time. Who might we become a year from now if we were to stop to name and pray for our enemies every week?

Worship as expression plays a much-needed role in our faith, and so does worship as formation. As is often true, the answer is both/and.

The second lesson John Witvliet taught us came right before we launched the first gathering of the Practice. After examining our ministry proposal, he said, "I see you using the words *formational* and *innovative*. Those words are not mutually exclusive, but realize that they are in creative tension."

The only way to form character, as well as a skill or habit, is to do the same thing over and over. We don't lift weights once and immediately have strong muscles. It requires repetitive action. Yet if we repeat the same action too many times, like lifting weights the same way without variation, we'll eventually hit the wall of diminishing returns. That is why we also need variety, creativity, and innovation.

Dr. Witvliet's counsel was "Choose a couple formational pillars of your liturgy that stay consistent for a whole season, and also create spaces in between for experimenting with new forms of worship." This is what we've tried to do.

WHAT IS LITURGY . . . REALLY?

Before diving into the pillars of the liturgy we use, it might help to first explore this potentially loaded word. What do you think of when you hear the word *liturgy*? Smells and bells? Dusty hymnals? Nothing at all?

When I attended church as a boy, *liturgy* was a dirty word. Or at least irrelevant. *Liturgy* was shorthand for everything wrong with dead religion. It was inauthentic, mindless, heartless, and rote. And it was opposed to the Spirit of God. Liturgy embodied the institutionalization of going through the motions, and I saw it as a dying horse that should be taken out behind the barn and put out of its misery. Liturgical churches were for cultural Christians who loved the church more than

God, tradition more than Christ, and rules more than the Holy Spirit. As you can tell, I was not a fan.

But as I joined with other Christians to explore beyond my experience of modern worship, we found that the depths were jam-packed with ancient practices and historic wisdom. The collective church had already been nearly everywhere we longed to go. In fact, the church had spent generations in places we had yet to even imagine. As I stuck my head under the surface, I was blown away by the treasures that I had known nothing about.

A quick example. We knew that a healthy worship culture would involve our whole lives—from celebration to mourning to spiritual gifts to our deepest sin. But all our songs were happy, and we didn't know the right way to bring our sin and broken-ness to God without it feeling trite or depressing. So like most evangelical churches, we avoided the idea of sin during worship, other than celebrating that we've been forgiven. We suspected this wasn't the healthiest approach but didn't know a better way forward. The historic liturgy, however, had already found this path and gave us the powerful tool of corporate confession. This text, from the Book of Common Prayer, is the confession we pray most often.

> Most merciful God,
> we confess that we have sinned against you
> in thought, word, and deed,
> by what we have done,

and by what we have left undone.

We have not loved you with our whole heart;

we have not loved our neighbors as ourselves.

We are truly sorry and we humbly repent.

For the sake of your Son Jesus Christ,

have mercy on us and forgive us;

that we may delight in your will,

and walk in your ways,

to the glory of your Name. Amen.[5]

This simple prayer—offered to God every Sunday—creates a safe and holy space in which we can name and hold our sin before God. Our sin is not the whole story, but it's absolutely part of the story. And as we speak these words together, we are reminded that we're not alone in our sin but carried by fellow sinners who are brave enough to step into God's merciful light. This beautiful prayer also gives us robust language to use for confession. For example, I rarely think to confess the things I have left undone, but each Sunday I am given the space to hold that possibility before God. "Loving God, is there anything you called me to do this week that I didn't do? Please speak. Your servant is listening."

After reading this confession together, we take a few minutes of silence to personalize the prayer and interact with our Creator. For me, this often involves naming the specific way(s) I fell short that week. Other times I simply sit in the silent weight of what God and I both know to be true. This silence has become one of the holiest moments of our worship service.

But the wisdom of the historic church will not let us stay there forever, and confession always brings us to an assurance of forgiveness. This has a different look from one Christian tradition to the next, but an assurance reminds us that we are already forgiven by God and our sin is not the end of the story. No matter what we've confessed, God's grace is bigger.

This is my favorite assurance:

> Receive the words of God from Psalm 103:
> "I am compassionate and gracious, slow to anger, abounding in love. I will not always accuse nor harbor anger forever; I will not treat you as your sins deserve or repay you according to your iniquities. For as high as the heavens are above the earth, so high is my love for you. As far as the east is from the west, so far have I removed your sins from you." (Paraphrase of Psalm 103:8–12 used in worship at the Practice)

COMING TO A MORE COMPLETE SPIRITUAL DIET

If we look at the story of Scripture, we can see the practice-based invitation from Genesis to Revelation. My friend and wise-beyond-his-years theologian John Perrine said it this way:

For those of us raised in a "belief" based approach to
the Scriptures, it might be surprising to discover that
practices actually formed the heartbeat of Israel's faith.
From sacrifices to festivals, from Sabbath to laws con-
cerning immigrants, Israel was given tangible practices
in the Torah on what it looked like to live their calling
as a "kingdom of priests" and a "holy nation" (Exodus
19:6). However, as the story progresses, the problem of
Israel's sin has affected the very practices themselves.
What once had been worshipful and transformative were
now either neglected or abused, empty props to be used
by the religious elite to mask their loss of faith in God.
So the prophets came to call Israel back from practices
that were ritualistic and meaningless to the very God
and kingdom those practices were always intended for.
When Jesus shows up, he goes even further by showing
us those practices of kingdom as they were always
intended to be, and then he invites us to "go and do
likewise" (Luke 10:37). This is the Story we've always
had but have sometimes lost, a Story that invites us to
join in the mighty river of God sweeping towards the
renewal and restoration of all things.[6]

One day as we ran errands, I was telling Shauna why the
historic liturgy was becoming so compelling to me. I rambled
on about liturgical formation (Passing the Peace, early Anglican

archbishop Thomas Cranmer, the order of service), and she jumped in and said, "It sounds like you're simply trying to offer a well-balanced meal." Yes! As usual, Shauna masterfully summed up my ten minutes of rambling in one perfect sentence. That was it.

For more than two decades as a worship leader, I had been serving just one kind of meal. This meal of singing four rock songs and a hymn was nutritious and good but only one type of food. It was only one part of the spiritual food pyramid, if you will. I had unwittingly helped create malnourished worshippers. Or to mix metaphors, have you ever seen those huge musclemen at the gym who have tiny bird legs? That is what we become without a well-balanced meal and a well-balanced set of practices: strong in a few areas and utterly powerless in others.

This doesn't mean that every church should turn into a traditionally liturgical church. We don't need to become stylistically Catholic or theologically Episcopalian or suddenly hang stained glass everywhere. This isn't about style but about form and intention. Do we have a plan in place to help form our communities and ourselves into Christlikeness? Are we feasting on and serving a well-balanced meal?

The word *liturgy* literally means "work of the people." It is the set of activities we do when we gather. Every church has a liturgy. The question is never "Do we have a liturgy?" but instead "How does our current liturgy form our community?" It's not about a certain style. Formational liturgy is not about old instead of new, quiet instead of loud, or sad instead of happy. Formational liturgy is all about participating in a holistic work of the people with God and one another that forms us into Christlikeness for the sake of the world.

For example, theologian and author Barbara A. Holmes observed in her wonderful book *Joy Unspeakable* that Eurocentric contemplative practices tend to be equated with individual silence, while Afrocentric contemplation tends to be communal and more varied in expression.

> If the model for contemplation is Eurocentric, then the religious experiences of indigenous people and their progeny will never fit the mold. But if contemplation is an accessible and vibrant response to life and to a God who unleashes life toward its most diverse potentials, then practices that turn the human spirit inward may or may not be solitary or silent. Instead, contemplation becomes an attentiveness of spirit that shifts the seeker from an ordinary reality to the *basileia* [kingdom] of God.[7]

Liturgy is not about a certain style. Depending on our cultures, history, or personalities, our "attentiveness of spirit" can be like a whisper or like a kick drum, found at a kneeler or through a praise dance. Liturgy is not about one specific aesthetic but about a well-balanced meal that forms us into who God has made us to be.

Worship leader and writer Sandra Van Opstal has taught that this well-balanced meal can find its fullness only in culturally diverse communities and worship experiences. Her powerful and much-needed book *The Next Worship* helps us notice the cultural framework within which we operate. Her writing helps us create a worship culture that both embraces and moves beyond our default cultural framework. In her words,

> Diverse worship allows us to stand in solidarity and experience mutuality so that we experience a fuller picture of God. This allows us to live into the reality that we are "one new humanity" (Eph. 2:15).[8]

A well-balanced meal should not be limited to the faith community gathered for worship. Rather, it is an expression of and movement toward the new humanity that Jesus Christ invites the world into. A diverse and well-balanced meal enables us to swim more fully in the eternally wide Current and makes space for every tribe, tongue, and nation to swim together. On earth as it is in heaven. Amen and amen.[9]

The invitation extends to our personal spiritual practice as well. Each day, in our private prayers, practices, and service, are we feasting on a well-balanced spiritual diet or do we keep reaching for the same small meal from the same few traditions?

THE LIMITS OF A QUIET TIME

Growing up in conservative evangelicalism, I was taught the importance of a daily personal quiet time. Every day—ideally first thing in the morning—we were to carve out fifteen minutes or so of solitude with God to read the Bible and pray. This was a time to get filled up with light before going out into a world of darkness. Being a responsible, achievement-oriented firstborn, I dove headfirst into this practice. From my junior year of high school through my postcollege years, I tried to read Scripture and write in my prayer journal every day.

This practice served me well in a thousand ways. I can't tell you the number of times God spoke through something I read. And more often, it took place in the holy moments as I journaled my heart out to God and *knew* I wasn't alone. I was a stoic Scandinavian male who was raised not to express many feelings. But my prayer journal became a safe haven where I could unload the really messy stuff on God. It was poorly written and often melodramatic, but it was as true to reality as I could make it. And in many ways, these prayer journals (which are all in a box in our attic) became the foundation for my relationship with God. I'm so thankful for this practice.

But a quiet time wasn't enough. At a certain point, I began bumping into its limitations. A quiet time could help me engage certain aspects of the spiritual journey, but it fell short in others. It was great for gaining concrete ideas about God and life but not very good at engaging the deep mysteries of God and life. My quiet time offered a brilliant place to read Scripture, apply it to my experience, and express my heart to God. But it didn't always *form* my heart beyond my natural perspective and proclivities.

Over time I realized that my quiet times were firmly in my own control. I did the reading, I asked God to speak, and I created and initiated the prayer response. Some of this was due to my immaturity, but some of the problems were inherent in a purely word-based practice. Words are wonderful and transformational, but they also are limited and limiting. Some realities are simply beyond words.

One of these realities is suffering.

MEETING GOD IN SUFFERING

Shauna and I have not experienced the level of tragedy that many of our friends have. But like everyone, we've had our hearts smashed to bits. One of our heartbreaks came the day Shauna was unceremoniously fired from her job at a church. I'll never forget the pain, confusion, and humiliation we experienced in the staff meeting when the leadership announced her termination. I stared holes in the floor, trying to figure out whether to run or yell or cry or burn the building to the ground. And then after the meeting, I had to walk back down the hall to my church office to figure out how to lead worship that Sunday. It was crazy.

For the next few weeks, I leaned into my prayer journal and poured out all the anger, hurt, fear, and hate I felt toward the people who had hurt my wife. At first, it was helpful to name my truest reality in God's presence. The tear-soaked journal pages were a holy first step. But after a while, returning to this journal didn't help. In fact, like lifting a bandage to check a wound, my quiet time became a barrier to healing. Episcopal priest and author Ian Morgan Cron has called this type of prayer pattern "rehears[ing] our anxieties."[10]

Almost in desperation, as Shauna and I walked out the door for a much-needed vacation, I grabbed a book my mother-in-law had given me a year earlier. It was *Open Mind, Open Heart* by Father Thomas Keating. This brilliant invitation to the Christian practice of centering prayer ignited something in my heart. To be honest, the fundamentalist voices still alive in the back of my head resisted the idea of centering prayer and anything else that sounded overly Catholic. Because I had been taught to be suspicious of anything "not from our pond," I tiptoed cautiously into the book. But while reading and listening, God's whispers of *Yes!* began to drown out the fearful fundamentalist shouts, and I decided to respond with a twenty-one-day experiment.

MEETING GOD IN CENTERING PRAYER

The Christian practice of centering prayer is a simple way to the "opening of mind and heart . . . —our whole being—to God, the Ultimate Mystery, beyond words, thoughts, and emotions," wrote Father Thomas Keating.[11] Rather than everything depending on my ability to verbalize or comprehend the spiritual experience, centering prayer offers a wide-open space where I can get my thoughts, words, and agenda out of the way. With all that set aside, God's still, small voice can finally be heard. It is a profoundly challenging and unbelievably transformational practice.

In that very painful season, I practiced this form of prayer for twenty minutes each morning for twenty-one days. Same time of day. Same basement room. Same brown couch. I'd begin with the Scriptures and then have a twenty-minute time of centering prayer. Then I'd journal about the experience. And let it be said: I was terrible at centering prayer. My mind bounced from thought to plan to worry to idea and back again. I rarely stopped to listen to God. Letting go of my attachment to my own thoughts was (and still is) embarrassingly difficult. But in the rare moments when the inner storm settled and God's light sneaked into the quiet, my life changed. Not all at once, but it really did—and in a way I couldn't have imagined.

The first two weeks of centering prayer were chaotic and healing and almost completely about God's work inside me. But a curious thing happened during the third week: I began praying for the people who had hurt Shauna. It was not my usual prayer of vengeance wrapped in pious language but a true prayer of blessing for their lives. I was being reminded of the fragile humanity that lay beneath their inhumane actions, and I simply agreed with God's infinite love for each of them. No kidding—my rage and hurt began to thaw, and I even had a couple of moments of truly letting them go.

To be clear, I didn't generate this prayer or decide to forgive the people involved. In ways I can't articulate even today, this work was done *in* me. All I did was make space and allow it to have its way. God's River of blessing and healing flows constantly in every corner and every moment. Our job is to notice the Current and learn to swim with it.

In a season of such pain, my former approach to having a quiet time could get me no deeper than the shallows. Believing that God's River involves forgiveness is irrelevant without a wise spiritual practice to help me swim with the forgiving Current. Words are important but not enough. However, the written Word (the Bible) plus the living Word (Christ Jesus) plus a practice that opens us to both written and living words (centering prayer) healed me. Does God still do miraculous healing? Absolutely. But we need to get into the water.

In the next chapter, we'll keep exploring what it can look like for fellow swimmers to gather to learn how to swim in the Eternal Current. We'll dig more deeply into one very specific example of what a practice-based gathering can look like in a local church. I think you'll be gloriously underwhelmed by how normal and unsexy it is. Yet I hope you're inspired by the holy possibilities of this and every community.

5

<hr>

Church as a Gymnasium (Part 2)

A Practice-Based Gathering

For the next few pages, would you join in a Practice gathering? Reading is not the same as experiencing, but I'll try to explain what we do when we come together, along with the intention behind it. Our engagement with practice-based faith is an attempt to align ourselves with Christ, get swept into the Eternal Current, and learn to swim for the sake of our lives and the life of the world.

And just to be clear: I don't believe that what follows is the one correct version of a practice-based gathering. Far from it. There are a million ways to learn to swim as a community, and there is no such thing as a one-size-fits-all solution. I humbly offer this chapter as a flawed but real example from a single context.

Each gathering of the Practice is broken into three parts: an opening liturgy, a teaching that leads into practice, and the Eucharist, which sends us out into the world. Gatherings are designed to open the community to the Spirit's presence among and inside us, to invite each person to move beyond belief into tangible practice, to make space to meet Christ humbly at the table, and to propel us out to join God in the world.

PILLARS OF FORMATION AND INNOVATION

In the last chapter, I mentioned that Dr. John Witvliet had advised us to "choose a couple formational pillars of your liturgy that stay consistent for a whole season, and also create spaces in between for experimenting with new forms of worship." Accordingly, we chose five practices to be the pillars of our liturgy, while also finding consistent opportunities to explore, risk, and follow the winds of the Spirit. Here are the five pillars.

1. The Lectionary

We align the opening liturgy with the Revised Common Lectionary, which is the schedule of Scripture passages that much of the church around the world follows. The person planning our liturgy begins by prayerfully reading through the four passages for that Sunday and asking, "What is the big story of these texts, and how can we join it?" The theme of these texts shapes the trajectory of the liturgy.

Following the big story told by the weekly lectionary readings reminds us that we are part of a huge, diverse, global family of Christ followers. We are reading the same biblical texts that millions of other members of Christ's body are reading on that day.

In addition, submitting to a bigger plan is both humbling and freeing. It shows us that novelty is not the church's highest value and frees us from the pressure of thinking up our own plan every week. Being a reinvent-the-wheel-every-seven-days evangelical can be exhausting.

Further, following the lectionary guides us through major sections of the entire Bible every three years. It situates our spiritual journey in the whole of Scripture, rather than the handful of sections that our community would naturally gravitate toward. The lectionary has been a huge gift to us.

2. Confession/Silence/Assurance

Another weekly pillar is the confession and assurance. Every Sunday night, we create time to hold our sin before God, sit silently in the weight of it, and hear an assurance of God's grace spoken over us. I can testify to the holy power of a weekly confession and assurance. (For more on this practice, see chapter 4.)

3. Singing

In many ways, music is the glue that holds the opening liturgy together. We try to choose from a wide range of styles—hymns, Taizé, old spirituals, modern worship, and others. And we sing pieces of songs more often than entire songs. The song is never the point, but singing serves the journey and helps us engage in a deeper way.

In many ways, the Practice uses music as a soundtrack of the liturgy. It accompanies the work of the people as the people pray, listen, read Scripture, and worship God together. We'll often have musical refrains that return throughout the service, tethering us to the theme of the night. Our community loves to sing together.

4. Prayers for the World

At least once a month, we dedicate a section of the opening liturgy to lifting up the needs of the world. Sometimes we use traditional "prayers of the people" from the Book of Common Prayer or a similar collection. Such prayers connect us to what the worldwide Christian family is praying that day. Other weeks, members of the Practice community write prayers that help us hold current events before God. And other times we include a time of open sharing in which anyone present can offer a specific prayer. Then we all reply with "Lord, hear our prayer."

Theologian Karl Barth famously taught that Christians should read both the Bible and the newspaper.[1] We are not of the world, but we are most certainly in it. We don't want our community to get overly isolated and forget about the bigger story. In very tangible ways, praying intentionally for the world helps us hold the two greatest commandments together as we worship: love God and love others. May it be so.

5. Space for Listening

We plan at least one space in the liturgy that allows people to notice what God is doing in them and then respond. My friend Sam calls these "planned moments of spontaneity." If we're not careful, worship liturgies can be packed with so many words and sounds and so much content and action that people aren't given space to notice and participate in God's work in them. It is possible for our sincere intentions to distract people from hearing God. So we carve out space to listen. Sometimes it will be one minute of silence following a Scripture reading to "let God speak to you through this text." Sometimes we follow the assurance with a moment during which people can thank God in their own words. Other times we'll offer an informal "Hey, I'm not sure what you need to say to God, but for a moment or two, while I play the piano quietly, pour your heart out to God." Our liturgies play a role in guiding the journey, but we also need to get out of the way.

These pillars anchor our opening liturgy and create a container for formation. But in the spaces between, we try to follow the winds of the Spirit and explore creative ways to engage God and one another. For example, while we always have an assurance after the confession, this moment can be the reading of Scripture, a song, or a poem. The pillars of our liturgy are unchanging (for a season), but we try to engage each pillar with creativity, openness, and experimentation.

We also feel free to introduce new practices or even to make up practices on occasion. Classic practices such as Lectio Divina, the Examen, and breath prayer are regular parts of the opening liturgy—often practiced in a modified or abbreviated way. And about once every quarter, Practice leader Kellye Fabian leads an extended time of praying for the world through images. Choosing six images of current events, she puts each one up on the screen, guides us in a short reflection that helps us see the person in the photo through God's eyes, and gives us space to pray for that person along with the systems that frame the person's story. It is incredibly powerful.

The key is to seek and share in a well-balanced meal. Rice, chicken, and dessert are a great meal, but you will not reach optimum health by eating this meal three times per day. At a certain point you need to add something green. And whole grains are hugely important for digestion. And healthy oils are critical. We can't eat from every food group at every meal, but a healthy diet must include a balance from every group.

A healthy worship gathering is the same. No one can do every kind of practice every Sunday. But over the course of a month or two, the community should have opportunities to engage the fullness of the human experience with God and one another. As a community, we need opportunities to feast on celebration as well as on lament and silence, thanksgiving and Scripture, intercession and mystery and poetry and improvised praise. We should be a space that comforts the brokenhearted and challenges the comfortable. God commands us to love God with our heart, soul, mind, and strength (see Mark 12:30). Expressive and formative worship liturgies can help expand our love for God in all these ways.

THE MIDDLE OF THE COMMUNITY GATHERING

Following the opening liturgy, we move to the second part of the gathering: a teaching that leads the people into practice. We approach this teaching in a couple of ways.

First, the speaker talks for only twelve to fifteen minutes. The time goes by quickly, which requires the speaker to focus on one thing—and focus quickly. This short time also decentralizes the role of the sermon in the service and decentralizes the personality of the preacher in the community. We don't allow enough time or space to overemphasize or overvalue the role of the lecture.

Second, the teaching is geared toward practice, not merely belief. We're not trying to change people's minds; we're trying to change the world. In our community, teaching serves to guide and propel us into tangible participation with God's work in us and through us.

The desired response is not "Yes, I believe that" but "Yes, I can engage with God in that way." A sermon can be a powerful springboard into concrete practices that open listeners to the Spirit's activity in a way that will transform them. God can use anything in any way to meet people, so we avoid being overly prescriptive. But we do throw our energy into teachings that lead to practice.

In a practice-based church, the teaching is crucially important but in a different way. As we discussed in chapter 3, without a clear vision of the kingdom of God, spiritual practices can range from having little impact to being destructive. As the Pharisees of Jesus's time illustrate, a practice-based religion without a kingdom theology is a terrible way to live. So teachers of the kingdom play a much-needed role.

Our good friend Mark Scandrette has influenced the Practice greatly in this way through his books, teaching, and mentoring. We often refer to him as the Godfather of the Practice. In the fall of 2016, he helped us create a nine-week journey through the Beatitudes called "The Nine Beats." His content was brilliant, but the most helpful idea he offered was the framework. Every week, regardless of the beatitude being taught, he showed us how to structure the content in four movements:

- What is the ache that this beatitude addresses?
- How do we tend to avoid and distract ourselves from this ache?
- What is the kingdom reality that Jesus offers to address this ache?
- What practice can help us align our ache with Jesus's kingdom vision?

These questions continue to frame everything we do on Sunday nights.

When the teacher is finished, another leader usually says, "Now let's practice this together." The leader guides the congregation in fifteen to twenty minutes of spiritual practice. Here are a few examples:

Following a teaching on God's deep love for each of us, a gifted pastor helped us soak in that reality through the practice of breath prayer. For twenty minutes, he slowly guided us to connect the words "God of love, I belong to you" to our breathing. Eventually we spent five minutes in silence to practice this form of prayer. The goal that night was not merely to believe in God's love but to experience it.

Following a message based on "Blessed are the merciful, for they will be shown mercy" (Matthew 5:7), I led our community through a four-step prayer to offer mercy to a person who had wronged us. I asked a question to frame the opportunity and then gave the people a few minutes to hold the question before God and listen. We continued through four questions and made space for God to do the deep work that only God can do. The goal was not to urge people to agree that showing mercy is good but rather to invite them to taste and see the freedom that comes from offering mercy.

During an Advent teaching about hospitality, the speaker, Jerusalem Greer, invited the community into a beautifully awkward practice. She paused in the middle of her talk and said, "Half of you have a bag of two cookies under your chair. Along with the cookies, I've included a short script that says, 'Advent can be difficult for me in this way: _____. I thought it might be difficult for you too. Do you want a cookie?'" As every introvert in the room prepared to sprint for the exit, she preempted us. "If you have a cookie, please stand up and find someone without a cookie and offer them the gift of hospitality." In this simple practice, we discovered connection that we couldn't have imagined.

These times of practice have deeply shaped our community. Not only do they help the content sink down into our bodies and souls, but they also create space for God to do whatever God wants to do. We've been consistently surprised and delighted by the unexpected ways the Holy Spirit breathes life into these moments.

But the most important aspect of a practice-based service is that we are mentoring and empowering people to practice all week long. Each time we learn a new practice, we add another tool to our holy toolbox. The people of the community don't have to wait for Sunday when the professionals will produce another event. We can create holy space anywhere we find ourselves. We can practice breath prayer as we sit in traffic with screaming kids in the back seat. We can pray the four-part prayer of forgiveness as we lie in bed after a painful day. We can take cookies to a hurting neighbor. We can live the way of Jesus inside or outside a church building. This is a beautiful thing.

The first movement of a Practice gathering is the opening liturgy. The second is a teaching that leads us into practice. And the final movement is the Eucharist and sending.

THE EUCHARIST

I already mentioned that the Eucharist (communion or the Lord's Supper or the table) is the high point of every gathering. I won't attempt to define or explain the mystery of what happens at the table. Instead, I encourage you to read Orthodox theologian Alexander Schmemann's book *For the Life of the World* and Father Ronald Rolheiser's book *Our One Great Act of Fidelity.* If you are unfamiliar with the depth and richness of a Eucharistic theology (as I was), these books are like portals into a new world. Read them slowly, reverently, and with great joy.

But even more important than reading about communion is receiving communion. If at all possible, find a spiritual community that helps you receive communion every week. It's that important. Here are a few reasons:

First, receiving weekly communion helps us return to Christ, over and over. No matter what else happens in the service, we land back in this central practice of the presence of Christ every week. After learning about lament, we bring our broken hearts into the presence of Christ. After experimenting with a new practice, we bring our destabilized selves into the presence of Christ. After celebrating God's goodness, we bring our overflowing gratitude into the presence of Christ. Rather than getting stuck in the concepts or information shared during a sermon or even in our own spiritual practice, we accept the invitation to bring whatever we're holding into the presence of the One who called us.

(Quick note: As discussed in chapter 3, we affirm that God is present in every place at all times. When we speak of coming to the presence of Christ at the table, we are scratching around at the mysterious way in which this sacrament opens us to the Christ who has been with us all along. I'm not suggesting that Christ "shows up" at the table in a metaphysical sense, although sincere Christ followers understand the mystery of the Eucharist in many different ways. But I am certain of this: *we* are empowered by the Spirit to show up to Christ in a deep way at the table.)

Second, even in a practice-based community, the weekly Eucharist reminds us that a practice-based faith is not ultimately about practice. It is about Christ. It is in Christ and through Christ and because of Christ that we risk getting into the River at all. Communion helps us keep the main thing the main thing. All is Christ.

Third, receiving the Eucharist every week transforms us into people who can humbly receive from God. Early in the life of our faith community, Ian Morgan Cron, an Episcopal priest, taught on the heart, theology, and practice of the Eucharist. It was mind stretching and heart forming. At one point, he provocatively declared, "Remember, friends, you never take communion." In a surprised and uncomfortable silence, he smiled and whispered, "It can only be received. Taking is what happened in the Garden of Eden. But opening our hands to receive will put the world back together."[2]

This imagery has forever formed the Practice community— both as we approach the table and as we approach the world. Week after week, as we humbly return to the table with our hands open, we learn how to receive from God. Slowly we are becoming people who can get out of our own way and allow God's River to bring whatever it may.

Finally, the Eucharist isn't the ending but the beginning. Roman Catholics refer to the Eucharist as the Mass, which is derived from the Latin word *missa*. *Missa* is related to the word *mission* and can be translated as "sent." The word *Eucharist* literally means "thanksgiving." Therefore, the Eucharist is a feast of thanksgiving that launches us into our mission in the world.

In his phenomenal book *Faithful Presence,* David Fitch articulated the deep connection between the Eucharist and mission. In answer to the question "How does God change the world?" he wrote,

> The Bible's answer to this question is the church. God's plan is to become present to the world in and through a people, and then invite the world to join with him. How does this happen? In the simplest of terms, a group of people gather and become present to God. In our life together, we recognize God in the presence of Jesus Christ through disciplines in which he has promised, "I am in your midst." By knowing God's presence in Christ in this way, we are then able to recognize his presence in the world. We participate in his work in the world, and his presence becomes visible. The world then sees God's presence among us and through us and joins in with God. And the world is changed. This, I contend, is faithful presence. This is the church. And this is how God has chosen to change the world.[3]

While Fitch suggests seven disciplines that help us tend to Christ's presence, he begins with the Eucharist. We practice tending to Christ's presence at the table each week so that our eyes are opened to Christ's presence all week long.

After receiving communion and singing "The Doxology," we say the same thing every Sunday: "Friends, Sunday is not the main event; our actual life—Monday through Saturday—is the main event." Then we offer "Kingdom Practices" for the coming week. This is a simple way to recast the vision of practice rather than settling for mere belief, to encourage the community in the name of Christ, and to share a few concrete ways to continue with a practice we learned during the service. To encourage this, we provide two or three minutes of coaching in ways to flesh it out in everyday life. This is very helpful in launching the people to keep company with Christ beyond Sunday.

Finally, in the spirit of sending, we stand up, open our hands, and receive a benediction that propels us back into our everyday lives. Whether through Scripture or poetry or our own words, the benediction proclaims,

> We've learned a new way to swim tonight; now put
> on your goggles and jump back into the water with
> Christ—who is always present and making all things
> new. We can be a part of God's healing of the world
> and healing of our own souls. Such amazing grace! Let
> us swim with these unforced rhythms of grace today,
> tomorrow, and every day. Go in the power and love of
> the Father, Son, and Holy Spirit. Amen.

6

Sunday Is Not the Main Event

A Practice-Based Life

The weekly gathering of the church is incredibly important for those who want to swim with God's River. No one can do it alone, and something supernatural happens when the whole body is together. God is creating a people on earth, not a collection of spiritual individuals, and the church is eternally important.

On the other hand, attending a church service is not even close to being the most important aspect of a spiritual life. An overemphasis on the weekly Sunday-morning event can do a disservice to the people of God. Overvaluing what goes on in a church service can actually diminish the church universal, the body of Christ.

How Overvaluing Church
Diminishes the Church

A church service takes up one or two hours of a week. There are 168 hours in a week, so life beyond a Sunday-morning church experience occupies the other 166 hours. Placing too much emphasis on a church service results, for many people, in de-emphasizing practice-based faith throughout the week. It's as if the one or two hours devoted to religious duty on Sunday takes care of one's devotion to God for the week. "Well, I got that taken care of until next Sunday."

Overemphasizing what happens at church also tends to assign too much importance to professional church workers. They have a role to play, to be sure, but their primary job is to launch everyone else into the remaining 166 hours of the week. Too many Christians have assumed that God's work on earth should be taken care of by the paid professionals, since they are the specialists in this field.

The church exists to equip the saints for ministry (see Ephesians 4:12). Ministry takes place primarily outside the walls of a church. Of the fifty-plus "one another" commands in the Scriptures, such as "Love one another" (John 13:34) and "Forgive one another" (Colossians 3:13), most can't happen fully while sitting in a church service. This is one reason we believe that Sunday is not the main event; our actual life—Monday through Saturday—is the main event.

What does practice-based faith look like Monday through Saturday? How do we swim with the River of God in every area of life—family, work, and relationships with our neighbors? Let's return to our central text:

> Are you tired? Worn out? Burned out on religion? Come
> to me. Get away with me and you'll recover your life.
> I'll show you how to take a real rest. Walk with me and
> work with me—watch how I do it. Learn the unforced
> rhythms of grace. I won't lay anything heavy or ill-
> fitting on you. Keep company with me and you'll learn
> to live freely and lightly. (Matthew 11:28–30, MSG)

When I first began to ponder this passage, the words *recover* and *take a real rest* captured my attention. I was weary, in part because I had been immersed in a form of Christianity that loaded more religious bricks onto my already-slumping shoulders. As a firstborn achiever, I carried them a long time, but my back was beginning to break. (It's interesting that religion often puts bricks on people's shoulders. The biblical story of the Exodus tells us that Pharaoh, not God, loaded people up with bricks. God rescued the people of Israel from the whole brick-building enterprise.) So reading these words of Christ felt healing, comforting, and deeply inviting. I could finally exhale in God's presence.

However, as our community meditated on this text, we

noticed that the invitation to rest accounted for only half of the invitation. Most of Jesus's words call us to action: *come, walk, work, watch, learn.* At first this seemed contradictory. But as we sat with the text, we began to settle into the reality that rest and work are far from opposites. In this context, they are the same thing—two sides of the same coin.

THE DUALISM OF DO VERSUS DONE

The dualism of faith versus works has wreaked havoc in my spiritual life. Teachers from Sunday school, summer camp, and beyond proclaimed, over and over, "It's not about what you do for God but what Jesus has done for you!" "There is nothing you could ever do to earn God's favor or blessing." Or as Martin Luther famously taught, salvation is by grace—plus nothing![1]

There is much to affirm in these proclamations. If we must earn God's forgiveness and grace with our good actions, then we have no hope. God gives us grace because God is gracious, not because we deserve grace. This is a foundational reality at the heart of the good news.

But if I'm honest, these teachings often left me feeling paralyzed. I was so afraid of slipping into "works-based righteousness" and so convinced that my righteousness was dirty rags anyway (see Isaiah 64:6) that I felt handcuffed from participating in my own spiritual life. Thankfully, Jesus did not share this one-dimensional understanding of faith versus works. Notice the way he ended the Sermon on the Mount:

> Everyone who hears these words of mine and *puts them into practice* is like a wise man who built his house on the rock. The rain came down, the streams rose, and the winds blew and beat against that house; yet it did not fall, because it had its foundation on the rock. But everyone who hears these words of mine and *does not put them into practice* is like a foolish man who built his house on sand. The rain came down, the streams rose, and the winds blew and beat against that house, and it fell with a great crash. (Matthew 7:24–27, emphasis added)

Jesus basically said, "In summary, do this. Whoever puts my teachings into practice will survive the storms of life." He didn't say, "Whoever believes that my words are true . . ." It is not just a matter of assenting to the rightness of certain teachings or affirming one's belief in the correct doctrines. His final teaching was *do this* if you want to live. The invitation is participation.

Dallas Willard, a brilliant teacher on the kingdom and spiritual practice, said it this way:

> You can be sure that if you do not act in an advised fashion consistently and resolutely you will not grow

spiritually. We all know that Jesus said, (in John 15) "without me you can do nothing." We need to add, "if you do nothing, it will be most assuredly without him."

Of course we must be concerned about works righteousness. I talk a lot about the value of spiritual disciplines but also the danger of using them as if they help us earn our salvation. But it is crucial to realize that grace is not opposed to effort, but to earning. Earning is an attitude, effort is action. Without effort, we would be nowhere. When you read the New Testament you see how astonishingly energetic it is. Paul says, "take off the old self, put on the new." There is no suggesting that this will be done for you.[2]

We have been invited into the River by grace and grace alone. There's nothing we can do to earn our way into the water. But the invitation is to swim, and that takes grace-empowered practice.

PRACTICE-BASED LIVING

What does this grace-empowered practice look like in our daily lives? Not every action is equally helpful, so how do we begin crafting a practice-based life, Monday through Sunday? I will offer four suggestions: we need a toolbox, a rule of life, a plan to help us throw off sin, and a commitment to engage messy, risky service.

1. A Toolbox

One afternoon, while meeting for spiritual direction with Father Michael Sparough, SJ, I mentioned that my daily quiet time was feeling really dry. I wanted to learn from his personal practice, so I asked what he does every morning. "There are a couple practices I follow every day," he said, "but for the most part, if I don't vary my prayer practice, I get really bored." He went on to describe the different ways he opens his day with God.

I am grateful that this godly priest admitted he could get bored in prayer. Me too. His humble honesty created space and grace for my relentlessly spinning mind. He met me where I was—rather than where I should be—and reminded me that I was neither alone nor hopeless.

Further, as he described the ways he prayed and practiced his faith, I noticed how many tools he had in his spiritual toolbox. All I had was a "daily quiet time," so my options felt scarce and binary: do a quiet time or avoid God. But Father Michael, in his robust Jesuit tradition, talked about prayer practices such as the Examen and imaginative prayer, Scripture practices such as Lectio Divina and the lectionary, different prayer postures that help a person open his or her whole self to God, ways to connect with the Creator in nature, and on and on. It was inspiring and helpful, and it showed me why my own tradition had felt so thin.

You probably have heard the saying "When all you have is a hammer, everything looks like a nail." Since my prayer toolbox had only one tool in it, I thought that my one practice should address every part of my spiritual life. But it couldn't. It was good but not enough to support the complexities of life and faith on this planet. We need to create a toolbox of spiritual formation.

Take advantage of accessible books that focus on historic (and modern) spiritual disciplines of the church. You could start with Ruth Haley Barton's brilliant *Sacred Rhythms.* Richard J. Foster's book *Celebration of Discipline* and Dallas Willard's book *The Spirit of the Disciplines* are classics. Others include Barbara Brown Taylor's *An Altar in the World,* Adele Ahlberg Calhoun's *Spiritual Disciplines Handbook,* Barbara A. Holmes's *Joy Unspeakable: Contemplative Practices of the Black Church,* Mark Scandrette's *Practicing the Way of Jesus,* and Tish Harrison Warren's *Liturgy of the Ordinary.*

While you are immersing yourself in the wisdom of these books, remember that the invitation is participation. Knowledge is essential to learn how to swim, but the goal is to get into the water. So my best advice is to experiment. Take holy risks. Try different practices for a set period of time and notice how they help you align with God's unforced rhythms of grace. If they do help, add them to your toolbox. If not, do some prayerful reflection about why not; then feel free to set the practice aside. No one can or should do every practice, but we all need a well-balanced set of practices.

Nathan Foster, author and son of spiritual disciplines teacher Richard J. Foster, told me, "When you boil it all down, each spiritual discipline is simply a slightly different way to offer our bodies to God as a living sacrifice." It really is that simple . . . and life changing.

2. A Rule of Life

Use this expanding spiritual-discipline toolbox to craft a rule of life. While I love dramatic and grand gestures, I'm finding that the key involves small, consistent practices. Engage the small stuff over and over. Extended retreats and heroic fasts have an important place, but they can't sustain a spiritual life on their own. I've needed to set up daily—and even hourly—guideposts that remind me who I am and whose I am. Even while working on a sermon or preparing liturgy, it is easy to step out of the flow of the River and do work apart from God's guidance and influence.

For many of us, it's helpful to create an intentional rule of life. Please don't be put off by the term *rule of life*. This simply refers to an "exterior framework for our interior journey: a kind of scaffolding to use to build the spiritual structure of our individual life with God." Pete Scazzero said, "It is an intentional, conscious plan to keep God at the center of everything we do."[3]

Every one of us has some type of rule of life—how we organize and spend our time and energy—but few of us have a holistic framework that will form us into the fullness of Christ.

To begin 2017, a pastor at the Practice, Jason Feffer, led the community on a six-month journey to discern and create our own rule of life. He explained, "A rhythm of life is a description of the life we long for and the disciplines we will practice to open ourselves to the transforming work of the Holy Spirit to close the gap between the life we long for and the life we are living." He suggested we build our rule on four relationships: with God, ourselves, our communities, and the world. We can't focus on all things at all times, but his insight is that every rule of life must engage all four relationships.

To begin discerning and crafting a rule of life, we need to get in touch with our deepest desires. These have little to do with seeking a career change or losing ten pounds but rather are the core desires that scratch around in our souls. We must get in touch with the whispers from God about who we are beneath all the fear and ambition and insecurity. Our deepest desires have to do with the glory of who God has perfectly created us to be. Until we can get in touch with those desires, our rule of life will be little more than a life-improvement plan or another set of New Year's resolutions.

Ruth Haley Barton, a spiritual formation guide to many of us, has explained it this way:

The ability to recognize desire and longing is the beginning of the spiritual journey because it opens up the possibility of choosing to order our lives more intentionally around what it is that our heart most wants. In this case we are talking about the spiritual longings of the heart—the longing for a way of life that works, a deeper experience of love and intimacy with God, deep and fundamental levels of change and transformation. Oftentimes we get in touch with these desires as we withdraw from the constant stimulation of life in our culture and allow more time for quiet reflection in our lives.

As we become quieter on the inside, we will become more aware of our deepest longings, and if we allow ourselves to become more aware, we can eventually make choices that are more congruent with our heart's deepest longings. This will include ordering our lives around the disciplines, values and relationships that we know will invite God's transforming work in our lives. Experiences of desperation—when our life feels empty or out of control, when a relationship is broken, when we recognize sin or negative patterns in our lives and don't know what to do about it—can also motivate us to order our lives in ways that will move us toward wholeness.[4]

Once we get in touch with the deep and holy desire bubbling up within, we hold that desire before God and ask God to lead us to craft a rule of life. For me, the idea of creating a once-and-for-all rule feels suffocating and overwhelming, so I commit to a time-bound experiment. I ask, "For the next three to six months, what concrete practices will help me close the gap between my deep longing and my lived reality in terms of my relationships with God, myself, my community, and the world?" This question can transform our lives if we enter deeply into the process with God.

3. A Plan to Throw Off Sin

If avoiding sin becomes the primary focus, our faith can quickly devolve into fear-based fundamentalism and we can become the very thing we're trying to avoid. The goal of the Christian life is not merely to sin less but to swim more. However, we must acknowledge how difficult it is to stay afloat in the Eternal Current when we are loaded down with the heavy weight of sin.

The writer(s) of the book of Hebrews advised,

Since we are surrounded by such a great cloud of
witnesses, let us throw off everything that hinders and
the sin that so easily entangles. And let us run with
perseverance the race marked out for us, fixing our eyes
on Jesus, the pioneer and perfecter of faith. (12:1–2)

To swim with Christ in the River of God, we must let go of the sin that sinks our soul. We don't do this to earn our way into the water; the love of God through Christ beckons us to come as we are. But as we wade deeper into the Current, we begin to notice all the different weights of the world around our ankles, wrists, and neck. For some, this is gnawing resentment that keeps us chained to the person who wounded us. For some, this is a secret (or not-so-secret) addiction that anchors us to a substance, activity, or late-night website. For some, this is a subtle but insatiable greed that binds us to our income, shopping malls, and credit cards. The human soul is easily entangled.

Merriam-Webster defines *sin* as "an offense against religious or moral law" or "transgression of the law of God." I respectfully reject these definitions as too narrow. Dallas Willard observed that many of Christ's teachings were not absolute laws to obey in order to avoid punishment but "mere observations about how life actually works."[5] Jesus wasn't merely trying to enforce God's law. He was trying to save us from the self-sabotage of sin. As Father Richard Rohr has said, "We are punished *by* our sins rather than *for* our sins."[6] So in this context, maybe a simple definition of *sin* could be "anything that drowns us or someone else."

Would you take a moment to notice the way(s) you are most likely to get entangled and drowned by sin? Especially when you are afraid, exhausted, or disappointed, what sin or "self-medication" do you find most enticing? Try to notice your usual pattern. And then spend some time asking God for eyes to see underneath this pattern. What is the unmet need you're usually trying to meet? What created the empty space, and how can you bring that emptiness into God's presence, rather than filling it in your own way? What most often stops you from swimming with Christ in the River?

4. A Commitment to Messy, Risky Service

Finally, a practice-based life Monday through Saturday must involve regular risk in serving others. We need to get our praying hands dirty.

When I was in college, the choir I was part of toured Europe for three weeks. Our choir director had encouraged us to study a book to learn some basic German prior to the trip, but most of us procrastinated and didn't learn much. This was not a problem until our first stop at a German deli. Suddenly we experienced the stress of not being able to communicate.

The bus ride that followed was unusually quiet because our noses were buried in English-German dictionaries. The theoretical need to know German wasn't enough to make us learn it before we left the comfort of America, but reality scared us straight. Reality has a way of doing that.

A practice-based faith is similar. We often begin in the safety of personal spiritual practices and comfortable circles, but we can grow only so much in these still waters. There are things we can learn only by moving into destabilizing reality. Reality has a way of exposing who we really are and how we need to grow. Simple answers and self-assured opinions can thrive in the safety of our insular experience, but stepping into the messy world with serving towels over our arms has a way of scaring us straight.

Psalm 24 declares, "The earth is the LORD's, and everything in it, the world, and all who live in it" (verse 1). A Sunday worship service is a crucially important subset of reality, but the whole earth is God's tabernacle. Every square inch of existence overflows with the holy potential of God's infinite presence, power, and grace.

In a great prophetic vision recorded in the Scriptures, Isaiah wrote,

> I saw the Lord, high and exalted, seated on a throne;
> and the train of his robe filled the temple. Above him
> were seraphim, each with six wings: With two wings
> they covered their faces, with two they covered their
> feet, and with two they were flying. And they were
> calling to one another:
>
> "Holy, holy, holy is the LORD Almighty;
>   the whole earth is full of his glory." (6:1–3)

The whole earth is flooded with the Eternal Current of God. Christ invites us to learn to swim in it for the sake of our lives and the life of the world. Where is this River? *Everywhere!* When does it flow? *Every moment!* What part of our lives is invited into this Eternal Current? *Every part!*

Yet each of us can see this sweeping reality from a single vantage point. We have a view of the River that is accurate but incomplete. Our swimming experience is true but profoundly limited. And this is why we need everybody.

7

We Need Everybody

Ecumenism

The more I retell these stories, the more I realize that I keep making the same point: my faith tradition is good, but it's not enough. You might be in the same boat. Your tradition (or perspective or family system or denomination) is most likely deeply good yet is only a part of the story. If you are like most of the people I meet, you have been offered profound gifts as well as profound blind spots.

Many of us, upon realizing the limits of our traditions, choose either to double down or to jump ship. We become loyal defenders of our "one true tradition," or we demonize our past and reject it and Christianity with it. Both paths lead to dead ends. We must find a third way.

A More Inclusive Way Forward

The spiritual concept of "include and transcend" offers a more whole way forward. Through this concept, we discover that the answer is both/and rather than either/or. Our past experiences are *both* crucially important *and* criminally not enough, and a healthy future must be built on our past as well as beyond our past.

Consider this in a linear way, even though reality is much messier. When we want to move from step 3 to step 4 on a journey, we often assume it requires a complete rejection of step 3 in order to move forward. (The stage that is most difficult to value is often the stage we just left.) But step 4 isn't a rejection of step 3; it's a more complete way that includes all four steps to this point. Remember that step 3 was the only way to get to step 4. But rather than stopping at step 3, we need to include it while transcending it.

It's important to invite all our previous experiences into a bigger and more holistic future. Choosing step 4 necessarily involves step 1 plus step 2 plus step 3. The point at which we find wholeness is the larger space called step 4. (I'm awkwardly scratching at the surface here. For a deep dive into the idea of include and transcend, read Ken Wilber's book *A Theory of Everything*.)

Or as Father Richard Rohr has said, "Everything belongs."[1]

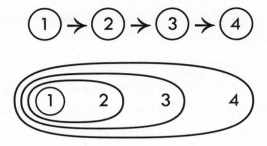

Consider this in terms of elementary-school math. As kids, we begin with addition and subtraction. Those foundations of mathematics *were* math to us. Then we learned about a little secret called multiplication and division. To our great surprise, our teacher explained that there was more to the math story, but our skills in addition and subtraction were needed as we moved into the bigger world of multiplication and division. We couldn't learn step 2 without first mastering step 1. So rather than rejecting our early math skills or refusing to grow beyond them, we brought these skills to new and bigger problems.

At an early age, we were taught to include and transcend. Multiplication is not a rejection of addition; rather, it is a bigger and more powerful way to add. Our faith traditions often require the same approach. For example, one of the first songs I learned in Sunday school was "Jesus Loves Me." If you grew up in church, you probably remember this one. And the idea that Jesus loves each of us personally is a wonderful truth for kids to sing. It helps them feel that they are seen. It helps form their sense of self and self-worth in light of God's abundant love. And it's absolutely true.

But the assertion that "Jesus loves me" is not the whole story. Not even close. The bigger story is that God, through Christ, loves *everyone*. God doesn't love only me, which is what the song helps us focus on. God loves me, my family, my enemy, and every person and family who ever has drawn a breath. "For God so loved *the world*" (John 3:16, emphasis added).

Some people, when they realize how small and tribal their view of God has been, decide to swing the pendulum the other way and reject the intimacy of songs and ideas such as "Jesus Loves Me." This comes at a great and unnecessary cost. Thankfully, the idea of *include and transcend* invites us to hold on to the early reality (that God knows and loves me) while bringing it into the fuller reality (that God loves everyone). If our only tool is either/or, we will be forced to choose between a smaller truth and a bigger truth. Include and transcend, however, invites us to bring the smaller truth into the bigger truth.

Christian wisdom teacher Dr. David Benner has written,

Identifying and embracing your lineage is an important part of any pathway to greater wholeness because it involves remembering your own story. All the parts of your journey must be woven together if you are to transcend your present organization and level of consciousness. For myself, the great challenge was reembracing traditions that I have grown beyond and that offered—even at the time—an oppressively small worldview. I did not want to be an exevangelical or an exfundamentalist. Too many people live that life of dis-identification, and I did not want to share their anger and "stuckness." It was essential, therefore, for me to identify and embrace the gifts that had come to me from these traditions. This was the way in which I came to truly know that everything in my life belongs, that every part of my story has made important contributions to who I am. And the same is true for you.[2]

What are the gifts that your spiritual (or nonspiritual) tradition gave you? What are the limits of your spiritual (or nonspiritual) tradition?

The concept of include and transcend is powerful precisely because most of us naturally default to include *or* transcend. Either we focus on the gifts of our traditions and ignore the limits, *or* we allow the limits to blind us to the gifts. We build big walls and refuse to learn from anyone outside our treasured traditions, *or* we reject all the things that remind us of our past and pursue only the new input that we feel repudiates our past traditions.

HOW TO MOVE FORWARD IN BALANCE

Give some thought to the way you tend to get out of balance. Do you naturally lean toward including without transcending or transcending without including? Do you get stuck in your known tradition and forget to learn from those outside, or do you easily reject your tradition and forget to learn from your roots? There's no shame in either tendency, and naming reality is the first step toward moving forward.

Ecumenism is one of the most helpful practices for learning to include our smaller story in God's larger story. This is a way to bring ourselves into the whole—to both learn and bless. The word *ecumenism* comes from the Greek οἰκουμένη (*oikoumené*), which can be translated as "the whole inhabited world."[3] Professor, writer, and founder of the ACT3 Network, Dr. John Armstrong defined it as "that which covers the whole planet, that which is of common origin and shares in that origin."[4] An ecumenical vision is humble enough to see the interconnectedness of all things and courageous enough to work toward this unity both in the church (see Ephesians 4:3; John 17:21) and in the whole world (see Matthew 24:14).

Margaret Rose, ecumenical and interreligious deputy of the Episcopal Church, has noted that ecumenism reminds us that "we're not the center of the world . . . and that God is just much bigger than our own definitions." And an ecumenical approach "helps us understand our own identity" and be radically recentered on "God's mission . . . [which] requires all of us to be involved."[5]

Ecumenical movements bring together diverse groups of Christians from all along the spectrum to dialogue and partner for the sake of unity, mutual learning, and fulfilling Jesus's prayer in John 17:20–23:

> My prayer is not for them alone. I pray also for those
> who will believe in me through their message, that all
> of them may be one, Father, just as you are in me and
> I am in you. May they also be in us so that the world
> may believe that you have sent me. I have given them
> the glory that you gave me, that they may be one as we
> are one—I in them and you in me—so that they may
> be brought to complete unity. Then the world will know
> that you sent me and have loved them even as you have
> loved me.

A good one-word definition of *ecumenism* could be "humility." Ecumenism helps us humbly receive and participate in the full reality of what actually is—so the world might know the One who holds it all together.

This is not to be confused with mushy relativism. We are *not* saying every idea is equal or every tradition is basically the same. Uniformity is a poor substitute for unity, because uniformity denies reality. In contrast, healthy ecumenism uncovers and celebrates the differences among us without allowing differences to come between us. In fact, when the Spirit of Christ is at the center, our differences become a blessing and a gift to one another. When we humbly submit to the reality that we are each an important part—but only one of many parts—of a bigger story, we can get swept into the glorious depth and width of the Eternal Current that has been flowing all along.

ECUMENISM AND A PRACTICE-BASED LIFE

Ecumenism keeps us in the Eternal Current in at least three ways.

1. It Opens Us to a More Diverse Practice-Based Toolbox

In the previous chapter, we discussed the richness in prayer that we miss when we settle into only one method of prayer. The same holds true for serving others and other spiritual practices. We can't eat the same meal every day and become healthy. We have so much to learn from other Christian traditions that will help us grow.

The Jesuit practice of the Examen reminds us to reflect on God's activity in our lives on a daily basis. The Anglican tradition gives us the freedom to compose our own prayers and also to get swept up in the written prayers of the church that have been handed down through the generations. The Book of

Common Prayer is an indispensable resource, guiding us into prayer paths that we might not discover on our own.

High-church friends offer the powerful practice of following the lectionary in community worship, as we saw in chapter 5. The Revised Common Lectionary can also serve as a guide for our private Scripture reading.

Father Thomas Keating, a Trappist monk, teaches the practice of centering prayer through books such as *Open Mind, Open Heart*. (Spiritual director and author Phileena Heuertz is another great teacher.) The gift of sitting with God in silence will open up new channels for God's Spirit to work in and through us.

Speaking of God's Spirit, Pentecostal and Charismatic Christians keep reminding us to cultivate moment-by-moment awareness of the out-of-the-box Holy Ghost. Spiritual practices are critical, but only if they are infused with the power of the uncontainable Spirit of the living God. As Jesus reminded the spiritual leader Nicodemus, "The wind blows wherever it pleases. You hear its sound, but you cannot tell where it comes from or where it is going. So it is with everyone born of the Spirit" (John 3:8).

Sabbath keeping, biblical lament, Lectio Divina, praying for the world, washing feet, inductive Bible study, Passing the Peace, the discipline of celebration, and on and on. These are just a few of the tools to be used in spiritual formation. Not every practice works for every person. But the wider Christian family offers a treasure trove for those who want to swim beyond the shallows of their own traditions and into the dangerous glory of the Eternal Current.

In the wildness and wonder of these deep streams, may we cry out with Saint Paul and all the people of God,

> Oh, the depth of the riches of the wisdom and
>   knowledge of God!
>   How unsearchable his judgments,
>   and his paths beyond tracing out!
> "Who has known the mind of the Lord?
>   Or who has been his counselor?"
> "Who has ever given to God,
>   that God should repay them?"
> For from him and through him and for him
>   are all things.
>   To him be the glory forever! Amen.
>   (Romans 11:33–36)

2. It Helps Us Balance Excesses

Author Ian Morgan Cron grew up Catholic, later pastored an evangelical church, and is now an Episcopal priest. From his deep ecumenical history, he often reflects on the difference between the Catholic imagination and the Protestant imagination.

Cron has observed that the Protestant imagination tends to

rely heavily on the discursive analytical mind. The emphasis is on transcendence and divine absence: God periodically enters history and then exits. Protestants tend to work hard at convincing God to show up.

The Catholic—or sacramental—imagination tends to be analogical and contemplative. The emphasis is on immanence: the world is brimming and overflowing with the abundance of God's glory in every moment.

Rather than arguing that one is more important than the other, we must understand that we need both types of spiritual imagination. "Each imagination offers us an important way to engage Reality," Cron has observed, "and each imagination helps correct the imbalances of the other."[6] This is yet another reason that we need everybody.

3. It Helps Us Become More Fully Ourselves

Getting outside our familiar traditions can help us go more deeply *into* our own traditions. This might seem contradictory, but it's not. Here's why:

- Being asked to articulate our beliefs helps us understand in a deeper way not only what we believe but also why. As we explain our faith to someone who has a different perspective, we are forced to abandon in-group jargon and speak plainly about our spirituality. Those with a different view don't share our assumptions, so we have to articulate exactly what we believe and give reasons for our belief. Learning experts suggest that we retain 5 percent of what we hear from a lecture but 90 percent of what we teach someone else.[7]

- Engaging "the other" with grace helps us become more secure in our own identities. We can be comfortable with the differences in others only when we're already at home with ourselves. Ecumenical work at times exposes how insecure we feel, but as we grow, it helps us feel more rooted in our identities.

- Healthy ecumenism helps us look at our own traditions and identify the flaws and the gifts through the eyes of a nonadherent. If we remain isolated from people who hold other views, we can lose perspective on our own strengths and weaknesses. A loving outsider can reflect reality back to us in a powerful and fresh way.

- Ecumenism helps us become more fully ourselves because it sands the ugliest edges off our faith traditions and offers tools to make our faith stronger. If we stay in loving and honest ecumenical relationships, we are left with versions of our traditions that are much more beautiful and holistic. Father Michael and I have commented on occasion that he makes me a better Protestant and that I help him become a better Catholic.

To receive the incredible gifts of ecumenism, we must cultivate at least two character traits. The first is humility, which I have mentioned already. If we are certain that we are already right, then we will be closed to others and unable to receive from them. Humility is a matter of life and death on the spiritual journey.

Second, we need discernment. The writers of the Scriptures encouraged us to sift and sort as we engage reality. In 1 Thessalonians 5:21–22 we are implored to "examine everything carefully; hold fast to that which is good; abstain from every form of evil" (NASB). The apostle John offered a similar teaching when he wrote, "Do not believe every spirit, but test the spirits to see whether they are from God, because many false prophets have gone out into the world" (1 John 4:1).

RECEIVING THE GIFTS OF ECUMENISM THROUGH HUMILITY AND DISCERNMENT

How do we hold on to humility and discernment as we hang in the holy balance? Here are four ways to engage ecumenical learning with winsome wisdom.

1. Build on the Three-Legged Stool

Father Richard Rohr wrote in *Immortal Diamond* that he built the book's teaching on the three-legged stool of Scripture, church tradition, and inner experience.[8] This strikes me as a helpful framework for discernment. As we approach a matter, we can use a similar three-legged stool. We ask,

- How does this align with my understanding of the teachings of Scripture?
- How does it align with the teachings of the wider church tradition?
- How does it align with my spirit as I pray and listen?

These questions will be interpreted through our own filters and personal experiences, of course, but the process of praying through them can offer a holy space for God's Spirit to illuminate and guide us.

2. Ask God for Wisdom

I'm not a super name-it-and-claim-it person, but James 1:5 has been a source of encouragement and faith to me over the years: "If any of you lacks wisdom, you should ask God, who gives generously to all without finding fault, and it will be given to you." At the risk of stating the obvious, whenever you need wisdom to discern something, ask God, who is *thrilled* to give it to you.

3. Look at the Fruit That Is Produced

The clearest way to discern whether something is aligned with God's Eternal Current is to look for the fruit. Jesus taught,

By their fruit you will recognize them. Do people pick
grapes from thornbushes, or figs from thistles? Likewise,
every good tree bears good fruit, but a bad tree bears
bad fruit. A good tree cannot bear bad fruit, and a bad
tree cannot bear good fruit. Every tree that does not
bear good fruit is cut down and thrown into the fire.
Thus, by their fruit you will recognize them. (Matthew
7:16–20)

A bad idea does not bring life and freedom, and good people do not cause constant pain and damage to those around
them. The way we do anything is the way we do everything.
But while assessing fruit is the clearest way to discern, it often is
the slowest way. Fruit can take weeks, years, or decades to grow.
Evidence is not always observable until well after we need to
make a decision.

4. Recognize That Discernment Is Not a Science

Finally, discernment is an art, not a science. It's not a math
equation that we solve. It's a conversation we join with the
Source of all wisdom. We engage it with our best thinking, our
trusted communities, and our whole hearts, but our faith is in
God's gracious guidance.

In the spirit of learning from those who have different traditions, different views, and different emphases from ours, let's

end this chapter with a well-known parable from India. You've probably heard a version of it. It often carries an interfaith message, which can be beautiful. But for our purposes, may this story invite us more deeply into ecumenical humility as we learn how to swim with Christ in the Eternal Current.

BLIND MEN AND AN ELEPHANT

In a distant village there lived six blind men. One day the villagers announced, "Hey, there is an elephant in the village."

The blind men had never encountered an elephant, so they decided, "Even though we would not be able to see it, let us go and feel it." They went to where the elephant was to learn what sort of animal it was.

They variously described it as follows:

"Hey, the elephant is a pillar," said the man who touched his leg.

"Oh, no! It is like a rope," argued the second after touching the tail.

"No, it is like a thick branch of a tree," the third man spouted after touching the trunk.

"It is like a big hand fan," said the fourth man after feeling the ear.

"It is like a huge wall," sounded the fifth man, who felt the belly.

"It is like a solid pipe," said the sixth man with the tusk in his hand.

They fell into heated argument as to who was right in describing the beast, each one sticking to his own perception. A sage heard the argument and asked them, "What is the matter?" They said, "We cannot agree on what the elephant is like."

The wise man calmly said, "Each one of you is correct, and each one of you is wrong. Because each of you touched only a part of the elephant's body. Thus you have only a partial understanding of the animal. If you put your partial views together, you will get an idea of what an elephant looks like."

It's important to note that not every approach to describing an elephant is valid. We need to avoid listening to some voices that would influence us. But those who have touched the elephant directly have a limited yet crucial role to play in helping the rest of us embrace the fullness of reality. Said another way, we are wise and blessed to listen, learn, and then share what we have learned from the diversity of wisdom and practice in the River that is God's kingdom.

This can happen only through proximity and engagement with those outside our tribe. The magic occurs around dinner tables and during service projects more often than in debates and white papers. We engage together, reflect on our experience, adjust for the new learning, and reengage. This can happen best in direct relationship with a diverse group of fellow swimmers who have a variety of perspectives and experiences. When sharing his support for ecumenical dialogue, Pope Francis commented,

> We must have a theological dialogue. . . . But this can't
> be done in a laboratory. We have to do it journeying
> (together), along the way. . . . We can't do ecumenical
> dialogue in a standstill. No. Ecumenical dialogue is
> done on a journey. And theological things are discussed
> on a journey.[9]

A sign hangs over our family's dinner table that reads, "Build a longer table, not a higher fence." These eight words remind us daily to be generous when we have more than we need, instead of clutching and hoarding. The words also implore our family and friends to include outsiders rather than choosing to protect ourselves from them. They need us. But more importantly, we need them. We need everyone!

8

We Can't Do It Alone

Practice-Based Community and Family

A few years ago, my wife, Shauna, signed up for the Chicago Marathon. It was surprising because Shauna would be the first to declare herself "a passionate nonrunner." But she took the challenge and joined the World Vision running team. Nine months later, she ran 26.2 miles and conquered one of her life goals.

How did she move from being a passionate nonrunner to being someone who could finish the Chicago Marathon? She had the benefit of a compelling vision, a clear plan, and a group of fellow runners.

Her vision to finish the marathon—both to achieve such a

feat and to raise money for clean water for kids, in partnership with World Vision—compelled her to rearrange her life around this difficult challenge. Without a compelling goal, there is no way she could have sustained such a high level of training for nine months. She also had a concrete plan. Many people throughout history have trained for marathons, and their collected wisdom offers a training schedule with a route to run every day. A passionate vision to run can get you on the trail, but only a time-tested plan can channel your passion toward constructive, lasting results. A vision without a plan begins with a bang but often fizzles out. Or it leads to injury.

Finally, Shauna had the support of a team of fellow runners. Every Saturday morning, the World Vision group met to do its "big run" together. Shauna told me later that not even one time did she wake up on a Saturday morning with a desire to run—and if it had been solely up to her, she probably would have hit the snooze button. But she knew her teammates would be there. She didn't want to let them down, and more importantly, she loved the connection with others who had committed to doing something so difficult. The vision propelled her into a wise plan that was sustained in community.

Friends, this may be the most succinct way to describe a practice-based life: it is a kingdom vision (swimming with Christ for the sake of the world) that propels us into a wise plan (spiritual practices that form a rule of life) that can be sustained only in community. We've talked a lot about a kingdom vision and a set of wise practices. Now let's turn to community. What does it mean to live a practice-based faith with others?

The writer(s) of Hebrews advised,

> Let us consider how we may spur one another on
> toward love and good deeds, not giving up meeting
> together, as some are in the habit of doing, but encour-
> aging one another—and all the more as you see the
> Day approaching. (10:24–25)

I'm not suggesting this can happen only in a formal church gathering. But in my experience, a Sunday gathering is one of the indispensable springboards for practice-based faith.

WHY GO TO CHURCH?

If you're like me (and pretty much everyone else on earth), you've had an imperfect experience of church. Legendary pastor and author Eugene Peterson has observed, "Every congregation is a congregation of sinners. As if that weren't bad enough, they all have sinners for pastors."[1] Or as the saying goes, "If you ever find a perfect church, please don't join it because you'll wreck it." Many people of faith have become disillusioned by even the idea of church. I feel that tension as well.

Eugene Peterson has also made this painfully honest observation: "There's nobody who doesn't have problems with the church, because there's sin in the church. But there's no other place to be a Christian except the church."[2]

We don't continue to gather on Sundays simply out of habit or to maintain a tradition. We gather as a church because God is creating a people, not just billions of individuals on independent, parallel journeys. Once again, theologian N. T. Wright has this to say:

> When [the apostle Paul] describes how persons, finding themselves confronted with the act of God in Christ, come to appropriate that act for themselves, he has a clear train of thought, repeated at various points. The message about Jesus and his cross and resurrection—"the gospel," in terms of our previous chapters—is announced to them; through this means, God works by his Spirit upon their hearts; as a result, they come to believe the message; they join the Christian community through baptism, and begin to share in its common life and its common way of life. That is how people come into relationship with the living God.[3]

In addition, gathering in worship helps us submit to something bigger than our personal preferences. We are invited to sing new songs, listen to new ideas, and follow a plan that often is not one we would have chosen for ourselves. As we are stretched, we learn how to find God's fingerprints beyond our preferred pathways. Learning to submit to something bigger than ourselves is an indispensable skill for swimming with the Eternal Current. Choosing to remain in isolation and complete control is choosing to stay on the shore.

Another significant reason to not forsake gathering as a church is that you are a part of the body (see 1 Corinthians 12–13). Since you are a body part, a crucial organ or limb or extremity of the body of Christ, the church needs you. The body is not complete without every part working together. God has given a spiritual gift to the church in you, and you dare not keep it to yourself.

Finally, a healthy church gathers a diverse group of people to journey together. Looking at things as a white, male, middle-class American has offered me one legitimate perspective among many. But I'm also finding it to be extremely limiting. There are many aspects of life and so much to God that no one can see from just one vantage point. Every one of us needs the broad, diverse perspective of the church.

Professor Soong-Chan Rah, in his masterful book *The Next Evangelicalism,* makes a case for why we need one another. He teaches that a theology of celebration is not complete without a theology of suffering. Resurrection is impossible without the reality of crucifixion, and crucifixion without the hope of resurrection is pure despair. Yet while Jesus lived and taught both, most of us spend our lives caught in the limits of only one side.[4]

For example, those of us who grow up with power, affluence,

and mobility often get trapped in a theology of celebration that keeps us mostly ignorant of the other side—suffering. And even when we try to bring our celebration into the suffering, the holy impulse to "bless the needy" can quickly lead to paternalism, arrogance, and seeing ourselves as the teachers rather than fellow creations and equals. This "hinder[s] genuine mutuality and reciprocity," according to Soong-Chan Rah.[5]

The poor are not problems to solve but teachers to learn from. They understand a part of reality that the affluent often can't see but desperately need to embrace, and vice versa. Both the rich and the poor are image bearers of God. Celebration is important, but it's only half the story. Without a theology of suffering, a triumphant story turns into a bad story. No matter who we are, we can see only one part of reality. We need one another. We need every one of one another.

While attending a church service is an important step into spiritual community, it is not the whole story. In fact, many of my Christian friends are also finding more spiritual life in living rooms, coffee shops, and other small gatherings.

LIVING ROOMS AND PRACTICE-BASED COMMUNITY

Confession: I have a complicated relationship with the term *small group*. I'm certain that a practice-based life can't be lived alone and convinced we each need a small group of sisters and brothers to help us swim in God's River with Christ. Yet when I think of a small group, I instinctively cringe.

Over the years, I've had a number of beautiful small-group experiences and have never been part of a train-wreck small group. Our house church in Michigan was life changing and heart saving in a hundred ways. A weekly breakfast with two friends has recently carried me through a very dark and scary season. The worship teams I served on began as serving groups and morphed by grace into transformational communities. And there are more examples. I'm grateful for the godly men and women with whom I've been able to journey. But the commonly understood framework of small groups can get in the way of the enormous potential.

Here's what I mean. A small group often has to do with only belonging or only learning. We desire either a place to be known or a place to study the Scriptures. Both of these desires are good and needed. The problem is, I don't believe that either desire should be the goal of a community. The goal should be learning to swim with Christ for the sake of the world. This involves putting Jesus's words into practice, not merely belonging to a group where we talk about them. The goal should be obeying Jesus's words, not simply studying them.

Imagine joining a marathon runners' group that met once a week to talk about what it takes to train for a marathon but didn't run together. You'd share life updates, but the question of "How did your running go last week?" would come up only occasionally. That's because for this group, training for the big race is not the goal. Belonging to a running group is the goal. Or imagine that your runners' group met weekly to read books about running but didn't go out running. That's not a runners' group. That's a book club.

I don't oppose belonging or learning, of course. I need to belong and to learn in deep and visceral ways. But they are the means to the end, never the end. One of my friends, Mindy Caliguire, often remarks, "Just because you are meeting with others doesn't mean you are in a transformational community."[6] And the goal of any group (or church or life) is to be transformed into Christlikeness for the sake of the world.

Reminding ourselves of the importance of *why* as discussed in an earlier chapter may be helpful here. Meeting with a small group is an incredibly important *how* of a practice-based life. Being in community is a matter of life or death spiritually. But when the *how* gets disconnected from the *why,* it can lose the plot and lose the power. So with the *why* clearly in view, let us roll up our sleeves to explore the *how* of community.

How do people form a practice-based community when gathered in a living room or around a dining-room table? They practice the way of Christ together, and they encourage one another to practice this way all week. The community is both the means and a beautiful benefit, but we never mistake it for the highest goal.

The activities of a traditional small group (sharing life updates, studying the Scriptures, praying for one another) can remain central to a practice-based community once everyone is clear on the goal. When we gather with a clear vision to learn how to swim in God's River with Christ, we then begin to discover the transformational power of the Holy Spirit through communal practices. And there are hundreds of practices.

Here are just a few of our favorite small-group practices.

One-Anothering

The Scriptures give us dozens of "one another" commands, including "Love one another" (John 13:34), "Live in harmony with one another" (Romans 12:16), "Wash one another's feet" (John 13:14), "Serve one another" (Galatians 5:13), "Carry each other's burdens" (Galatians 6:2), and "Forgive one another" (Colossians 3:13). It's challenging when you realize that almost none of the commands can be fully obeyed in a traditional church gathering.

If we desire to live in the way of Jesus, we need to expand our worship from being shoulder to shoulder (sitting in an auditorium or sanctuary facing a stage or pulpit) to being face to face. Consider reading through all the "one another" commands with your community and humbly asking, "How are we doing? In what areas of one-anothering are we doing well?

In what areas do we need to keep working?" These can be named while attending a church service, but they can be lived and fleshed out only in community, which works best in smaller groups. We cannot live the way of Christ alone.

A living-room meeting of a small group is also a space for true spiritual listening. Sibyl Towner—a teacher, spiritual director, and mentor to many of us—loves to quote David Augsburger: "Being heard is so close to being loved that for the average person they are almost indistinguishable."[7] She has helped us realize that the safe spaces of listening are rare, incredibly formational, and completely possible if we submit to a few simple guidelines. Check out Sibyl's training on "3-Way Listening" in the One Life Maps resources.[8] The simple framework will transform your living room into a holy space.

Dietrich Bonhoeffer, a German pastor and theologian, wrote,

The *first* service one owes to others in the community
involves listening to them. Just as our love for God
begins with listening to God's Word, the beginning
of love for other Christians is learning to listen to them.
God's love for us is shown by the fact that God not only
gives us God's Word, but also lends us God's ear. We
do God's work for our brothers and sisters when we
learn to listen to them.[9]

Confession

A living room serves as a powerful space within which to confess our sins to God through another person. The Scriptures repeatedly link our engagement with God to our engagement with one another. Here are two examples.

> Confess your sins to each other and pray for each other so that you may be healed. The prayer of a righteous person is powerful and effective. (James 5:16)

> If you forgive other people when they sin against you, your heavenly Father will also forgive you. But if you do not forgive others their sins, your Father will not forgive your sins. (Matthew 6:14–15)

God could heal or forgive us directly without involving other people, right? Why does God consistently work in us through our flesh-and-blood communities? Dietrich Bonhoeffer in his book *Life Together* engaged this question head on, suggesting that our personal confession can devolve into confessing to and absolving ourselves, while confessing to another Christian breaks the circle of self-deception: "Those who confess their sins in the presence of another Christian know that they are no longer alone with themselves; they experience the presence of God in the reality of the other."[10]

Praying Through Christ

In addition to confession, there is prayer. A community is the fullest way for us to pray through Christ. Father Ronald Rolheiser wrote this in his life-changing book *The Holy Longing:*

> As Christians, we have a set formula for ending all of our prayers—"We ask this through Christ our Lord." This formula is more than a formality, a ritual signal to God that the prayer is over. When we pray "through Christ" we are praying through the Body of Christ, which then includes Jesus, the Eucharist, and the body of believers (ourselves) here on earth. We are praying *through* all of these. Thus, not only God in heaven is being petitioned and asked to act. We are also charging ourselves, as part of the Body of Christ, with some responsibility for answering the prayer. To pray as a Christian demands concrete involvement in trying to bring about what is pleaded for in the prayer.[11]

This very Catholic teaching may stretch some Protestants. But consider a simple example: If someone in your community is desperately lonely and you pray that God would meet the person's loneliness through Christ, is it possible that *you* are God's answer? Can you sincerely pray, "God, please send someone to my friend!" while you stay at home? If we truly are

Christ's hands and feet on earth, when we open our hands to pray, we're also opening our hands to serve.

A PRACTICE-BASED FAMILY

Our families provide us with yet another powerful venue for a practice-based life. In a hyperseparated world where even many churches separate us according to age groups on Sunday mornings, the home can be a powerful greenhouse for spiritual formation. In fact, some say that the family is the *primary* place for discipleship, while church gatherings and outside services merely support what goes on at the central spiritual gymnasium of the home.

Shauna and I have recently begun to incorporate spiritual practices into our family life, and they have already been powerful. Here are some first steps you can take toward the goal of a practice-based family.

First is a daily Examen that Shauna and I simply call "high/low." Most days, usually at dinner, we go around the table so each family member can share a high of the day. This is a part of the day when we felt most alive, grateful, and connected to God. Then we share our low, when we felt sad, scared, or disconnected.

When our younger son, Mac, was three-ish, most of his high/low moments involved dragons, flying, or some other fictional adventure. But now that he's six, he often shares something from his day. Our eleven-year-old son, Henry, leans into this practice in an earnest and sometimes profound way.

This "family Examen" reminds us to stop, look back, and review our days. It helps us notice the goodness and blessings in even the most mundane or difficult days. It creates a safe space to bring up the difficult moments of life, rather than pretending all is well or waiting for a crisis before we talk about things. And the Examen creates a daily opportunity to notice God's fingerprints on our relationships, playgrounds, work emails, and everything in between. I think Saint Ignatius might have been onto something.

Second, Shauna reads with the boys most nights, exposing them to the story of God through two books in particular, *The Advent Book* and *The Jesus Storybook Bible.* Both books have created intentional and holy space for spiritual conversation with our boys that would not have otherwise happened. The importance of shared language and shared stories in a family cannot be overstated.

Third is the Lord's Prayer. Father Michael taught the Practice community a way to pray the Lord's Prayer with our bodies, using simple gestures. "When you pray," Father Michael has said while teaching about embodied prayer, "say to God with your body what you're saying with your heart and mind. We are not brains on a stick but fully embodied images of our Creator."

Our little family prays this form of the Lord's Prayer every night, motions and all. The boys love it, and Shauna and I often fight back tears. It is a simple yet incredibly powerful way to embody, literally, the words of Jesus.

Fourth, we're exploring ways to engage the needs of our community and world as a family. This has been harder for us to figure out compared with our at-home spiritual practices, but we're committed to creating a shared family mission.

The Practice-Based Family and the Church Calendar

One of our friends, Jerusalem Greer, an author and lay minister in her Episcopal church, has been leading her family in spiritually formative practices in the home. She has said the church calendar has been the key. Since she's further down the road on this journey, I'd love to end this chapter by sharing a conversation between us.

AARON: Why do you believe so much in practicing together as a family based on the church calendar?

JERUSALEM: I did not grow up in a liturgical Christian tradition, but by my midtwenties . . . I found that I was attracted to—craved, even—the rhythm, internal and external, that liturgy seemed to bring to those who leaned in and embraced it.

Once a new mom, I set out to find a way that would create traditions of faith for our family through the rhythm of the liturgical calendar, using fun, modern, colorful crafts and recipes, hoping to create experiences and gatherings that would tether myself and my kids to God's story. I wanted to find a way to create a deep sense of belonging in my children, a sense that they belonged to God, to the community of believers, and to humanity. By celebrating feast days of the saints or high holy days such as Pentecost at home, I hoped to help my kids (and myself) come to understand just how connected we all are to each other. No one's story or life happens in a vacuum. Our experiences, failures, and successes are all interwoven. And there is so much richness and understanding to be found in learning about and connecting to the stories of Christ followers throughout the centuries.

When we celebrate the liturgical year at home—diving deep into the lessons learned and wisdom shared by the people of God—we find a wealth of support, encouragement, and solidarity. The liturgical calendar helps us to remain tender to the continuing needs of humanity and the continuing work of the Holy Spirit. It connects us to the stories and lives of others—past, present, and future—through its rhythms and patterns. You see, within the liturgical calendar there are seasons of repentance, rest, celebration, and new life. There are days to remember the deaths of children, gone too soon. Days to give thanks for the harvest of our gardens and days to honor the sacrifices made by our faith ancestors, who can all teach a thing or two about discipleship. There are traditions that remind us to be a light in the darkness, that teach us about sacrifice, that encourage us to share our abundance. There are days when we remember our baptisms, when we pause to give thanks for the ability to give thanks around the table, and when we honor the majesty of Christ.

The calendar provides us a rhythm through which we can practice the full human experience through the redemptive lens of grace.

AARON: What does all this look like?

JERUSALEM: After a lot of trial and error, our family has come upon a few regular practices and a few occasional ones.

Advent kicks off the church year, and it was the first practice we began to observe regularly as a family when the boys were little. We have an Advent wreath patterned after the ones of my Alaskan childhood. (Everything you need to create this Advent wreath

with your family can be found in *A Homemade Year*.)
We follow the same schedule of lighting [Advent
candles] and [doing the] readings. In the beginning,
Nathan [my husband] and I did the reading and the
boys did the candle lighting and extinguishing. But as
they have grown, so has their ability to participate in
the readings and prayers.

But . . . it took ten years before celebrating these
practices wasn't awkward anymore. For the first nine
years, we had limited success in terms of participation,
excitement, and buy-in. But in the tenth year it all
suddenly came together. No arguing, no resistance,
no eye rolls. Everyone helped, everyone enjoyed it,
and everyone was present to the experience. This is a
once-a-year practice that resembles no other practice in
our modern lives. Why would it seem natural the first
half a dozen tries? So my advice to anyone trying the
Advent wreath or any other new home[-based] faith
practice is this: keep going. Don't stop because it was
hard one time. Don't stop because it was hard nine
times. Keep trying. It will click. Also remember, just
because [the kids] grumble or act like they don't like it,
[that] doesn't mean it isn't doing the formation work it
needs to do. A lot of kids don't like brushing their
teeth either.

When the kids were little, we also did an Advent garland countdown pretty religiously. As they have gotten older and our lives more spread out, it became obvious that the wreath and not the garland was the more meaningful experience for our family. So we let the garland die out.[12]

Every one of us, whether training for a marathon or learning to swim in the River of God for the sake of the world, needs a vision, a plan, and a community. The first two without the third won't get us there. We can't do it alone.

As we learn to swim, not just on Sunday but all week long, the Eternal Current begins to sweep us into participation with God's heart and mission: the redemption and flourishing of all things. Which brings us to my favorite chapters in this book.

9

For the Sake of the World (Part 1)

Practice-Based Mission

Have you ever had a moment that broke your heart and launched you into a new mission? I've had only a few experiences such as this, but one happened a few years ago in a basement conference room in Washington, DC. The room had bad fluorescent lighting, and much like God spoke to Moses through a burning bush, I think God may have spoken to me through the buzzing overhead tubes.

A couple of years earlier, in 2010, I had joined a group of leaders on a ten-day trip to Israel and Palestine. Beyond sightseeing and spiritual pilgrimage, we learned from peacemakers on both sides of the conflict. I was already aware of the Israeli part of the story, but the Palestinian reality was new to me. And overwhelming. Traveling in Israel and Palestine was one of the most moving, stretching, horrifying, and inspiring experiences of my life. It has continued to shape me over the last decade.

Not long after the trip, I met Todd Deatherage and Greg Khalil, who had founded the Telos Group. Todd, an evangelical from Arkansas, had worked in the US State Department during the George W. Bush administration. Greg, an American of Palestinian descent, is a lawyer who advised the Palestinian government during peace negotiations. While emerging from seemingly opposite sides of the Israeli-Palestinian issue, both men believe that "peace in the region [is] vital to America's national security interests, that a sustainable solution to the conflict [will] never be achieved without strong, bipartisan support from the United States, and that such support [will] not materialize unless and until Americans—and especially Americans of faith—[become] truly committed to the security, freedom, and dignity of both Israelis and Palestinians."

Greg and Todd have thrown themselves into "educating, inspiring, and equipping key American communities to actively pursue the common good for everyone in the Holy Land." They are building a pro/pro/pro movement: people who are pro-Israeli, pro-Palestinian, and pro-peace.[1]

I joined them on three trips to Israel and Palestine and found that Telos is doing some of the most important work on earth. That's not hyperbole. Not only are they working toward a just and lasting peace for Israel and Palestine, but they are also inviting American Christians to put the Prince of Peace's words into action.

At a Telos conference in 2012, underneath the buzzing fluorescent lights, conferees were asked to break up into groups by religion: Christian, Muslim, and Jewish. Within the Christian group, people were separated into Catholic, Protestant, and Eastern Orthodox subgroups. In my smaller Protestant circle, we reflected on the question "How can I invite my community at home into this pro-Israel, pro-Palestinian, pro-peace conversation?" It was fascinating to hear an Episcopal priest talk about a peacemaking liturgy from the Anglican tradition. It was great to hear how a Lutheran pastor was preaching about God's peace-bringing kingdom. Then the conversation turned to me. With my heart racing, I tried to articulate what was bubbling inside me.

> I'm beginning to realize that every Sunday, as white American evangelicals, we accidentally but actively form one-sided people. Our songs are primarily triumphant and often animated by an undercurrent of "us versus them." The sermons tend to avoid ambiguity and doubt and [instead] focus on ways to defend our rightness against the wrongness of others. Our services avoid silence, lament, and self-reflection at all costs. And we've eliminated most of the spiritual practices

that make people feel uncomfortable—confession, praying for our enemies, and so on—which tend to be what God uses to break us out of our smaller stories.

I'm worried that there is no way to bring a pro-Israeli, pro-Palestinian, pro-peace conversation into such a narrow expression of faith. If our framework forces us to always choose one side against another, then the resulting question can only be "Who is the good guy and who is the bad guy?" Beginning with this dualistic question eliminates any space to engage the messy complexities of a real conflict and thus eliminates any way to discover what could make for peace. My evangelical tradition is largely not ready to engage this conversation until we get back into the business of spiritual formation. Our church is fantastic at manufacturing American Christians, but we don't have a pathway in place to make disciples of Jesus for the sake of the world.

When I stopped talking, the others in the circle looked at me with kind eyes. But no one said a word because they knew enough about white evangelicalism to know that I was onto something.

For the next hour, in the newly broken soil of this realization, God began to plant seeds. As my heart burned and I wrote furiously in a notebook, a new calling began to emerge: I needed to create liturgies, songs, and prayers that would help grow "us versus them Christians" into "both/and Christ followers." For the first time, God was giving me eyes to see how a passion for spiritual formation wasn't opposed to a passion for mission and peacemaking—rather, these passions are two sides of the same coin. In fact, without being formed into Christlikeness, we cannot sustain the difficult work of mission. Unless we learn how to swim, we will drown when the River carries us to the tumultuous shores that most need us.

In the same way that effective swimming requires both our left arm and our right, spiritual formation and mission are deeply connected for those who long to get swept up in the Eternal Current. Without both, we'll merely swim in circles.

INTERCONNECTED PEOPLE, PRACTICES, AND LENSES

In many Christian contexts, we separate discipleship from mission and evangelism from community. We create a discipleship silo for the introverts, a mission silo for the bleeding hearts, an evangelism silo for the connectors, and a community silo for the party people. The problem, however, is that they are all part of the same story. A healthy spirituality will integrate every aspect of faith into a holistic, interdependent organism rather than splitting the spiritual life into separate, autonomous pieces. Discipleship is not an optional add-on to evangelism. Mission is not an optional add-on to discipleship. The spiritual life is not a Ford Motor Company assembly line. Instead, the Eternal Current is a beautifully messy journey experienced through interconnected people, practices, and lenses.

One of the great gifts of Ignatian spirituality is that it honors the connections. It never separates our inner world from our outer actions. Saint Ignatius taught his followers to be "contemplatives in action" rather than to concentrate exclusively on contemplation or action. We engage the spiritual life as a spiral through three interrelated postures: beliefs, action, and reflection/prayer. Our beliefs propel us into tangible action that creates an experience—both inside us and in the outside world. We humbly bring this experience to God in reflection and prayer, receiving God's perspective, healing, and strength. Once grounded in God's grace and power, we are propelled back into the world through action, which continues the spiral. As we grow in Christ, the spiral gets tighter and tighter, sewing action and contemplation into a seamless garment and drawing us closer to the heart of God.

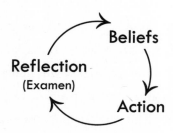

Many others have been inviting people of faith to follow Jesus's example of "contemplative activism" for the sake of the world. Phileena and Chris Heuertz formed the Gravity Center for this reason. They work to ground "social change in contemplative spirituality, *to do good better,* by facilitating contemplative retreats, spiritual direction, and enneagram consultations."[2]

In *Pilgrimage of a Soul,* Phileena Heuertz wrote,

> The union of action and contemplation brings freedom and joy—even in the midst of some of the greatest poverty and suffering of our time. By abandoning ourselves regularly to God through prayer in the form of solitude, silence and stillness, we experience more freedom *from* compulsions and heavy-laden expectations and more liberty *in* our true self with all of our unique gifts to offer the world. Bringing balance to action and contemplation in our lives allows for the greatest impact in our world. And the love of God compels us to not lose heart in the journey.[3]

Bethany Hoang is a contemplative activist who has served with International Justice Mission (IJM) for more than a decade. She engaged some of the most difficult and heart-wrenching justice issues on earth and now helps leaders around the world connect justice and spiritual formation.

Talking about her book *Deepening the Soul for Justice*, Bethany reminded us that the work of justice can be overwhelming. Crushing, even. To engage the horrors of young girls in sex slavery, for example, can be more than a human heart can bear. But she pointed out,

> To move into the crushing reality of injustice with hope, with joy, and with strength—that only comes when we enter it with Jesus. We can only enter with Jesus when we have opened ourselves to his presence and to what he has to give us, and that "opening" of ourselves is what spiritual disciplines enable us to do.[4]

We don't have to choose to be either exhausted activists or isolated contemplatives. In fact, to choose only one is to ultimately choose neither, because the inner journey and the outward journey are the same thing. The way we do anything is the way we do everything, as Father Richard Rohr has stated.[5] We can't separate spiritual formation from God's redemptive mission in the world because our spiritual formation is part of God's redemptive mission. Or as my wife, Shauna, has said, "If you sacrifice your body and soul to build God's kingdom, then you are actually damaging God's kingdom—because your body and soul are part of it!"

Jesus Christ invites us to leave behind our exhaustion and isolation and to live in the unforced rhythms of contemplative activism. Christ invites us not just to believe about the River of his kingdom but also to learn to swim with it for the sake of others. But what does this mean in such a broken world? What does it look like to practice mission that embodies and extends unforced rhythms of grace to others? Let me offer four practices for our personal lives. (Later I'll suggest three practices for faith communities.)

ENGAGE THE INWARD AND THE OUTWARD

Our rhythm (or rule) of life must invite us both inward and outward. The key is to create intentional space in our lives for contemplative practices *and* practices of activism. Depending on your personality, you naturally lean one way or the other. This is good. But with that in view, we all must structure our lives in ways that engage both directions.

As an introvert, continue with centering prayer and journaling, but also show up once a week at a homeless shelter. Your prayers will deepen tremendously as you engage Christ in the other. If you are a natural activist, keep serving. But also structure consistent times of silence, introspection, and prayer. You will have so much more to give to the world if you show up with a vibrant and grounded soul.

Would you reflect on this for a moment: Does my life naturally lean outward (without enough inward grounding), or does it naturally lean inward (without enough outward engagement)?

What is one practice I could add to bring a fuller both/and balance?

DIVERSIFY

One of the most practical ways to open up to God's active work in the world is to diversify our social-media feeds, friendships, and partnerships. Nothing creates complacency like living in a bubble. And conversely, nothing fuels an us-versus-them mentality (which usually swims against the current of God's redemptive work) like living in a bubble. Here are a few questions to consider:

- Do I get most of my news from one source, or do I actively access multiple news outlets?
- Do I find that my whole Facebook and Twitter feeds tell basically the same story?
- Do I primarily hang around with people who vote the same way, talk the same way, and believe the same way?

We can pursue diversity ideologically, religiously, and politically, which are all extremely important. But let me be really honest. The last few years have stretched me to acknowledge how culturally and racially homogeneous my life has become. Even though I've been learning from liberals and conservatives, Catholics and Protestants, women and men, religious and antireligious, it hit me that my "diverse" group of influencers was primarily white. And no matter how many traditions were represented, the overwhelming whiteness has prevented me from seeing a large segment of the story. I'm making major changes in my life and ministry, and I want to set a new trajectory for the rest of my life. We cannot engage or even understand the fullness of the kingdom of God from only one cultural perspective. I have so much to learn, unlearn, and relearn.

What about you? What areas of your life tend to be most open to a diverse range of influences, and what areas tend to feel a bit closed and homogeneous?

Here are a few steps we can take to keep learning from a wider community:

- Again, take an inventory of your social-media feeds. Do they primarily reflect one cultural cohort and one racial demographic and bias?

- Look through your bookshelf and Kindle. Are the books written primarily from a homogeneous socioeconomic and ethnic perspective? Or are you learning from a wide range of cultures and writers? (Personally, I was shocked to realize that an overwhelming percentage of books on my shelf were written by white European men.)

- Do the phone test. Racial-reconciliation leader David Bailey, who is a friend of mine, has suggested that we check our phone's call history. How diverse are the last ten people you called? If they are not, what does that say about your social circle? How can you expand this circle?

- Speaking of David Bailey, his ministry, Arrabon, is doing incredible work to create art and culture for a reconciled world and also to teach and train people who want to become reconcilers in their everyday lives. Check out Arrabon's deeply needed work at http://arrabon.com.

- Consider the organizations with which you partner. Does everyone look like you, or do you link arms with people from a wide range of cultural, socioeconomic, religious, and racial backgrounds?

Pray, Forgive, and Love

Actively pray for and show love to the people in your life who drive you crazy. God is redeeming and restoring *all* things. That includes our most difficult and broken relationships. We can't participate in the healing God wants to bring "out there" if we're unwilling to participate in the healing God wants to bring to our most intimate stories, relationships, and wounds. The way we do anything is the way we do everything. And a very helpful litmus test for the health of our soul is how we engage those who have hurt us.

Consider Jesus's words:

You have heard that it was said, "Love your neighbor
and hate your enemy." But I tell you, love your
enemies and pray for those who persecute you, that
you may be children of your Father in heaven. He
causes his sun to rise on the evil and the good, and
sends rain on the righteous and the unrighteous.
(Matthew 5:43–45)

To you who are listening I say: Love your enemies,
do good to those who hate you, bless those who curse
you, pray for those who mistreat you. If someone slaps
you on one cheek, turn to them the other also. If
someone takes your coat, do not withhold your shirt
from them. Give to everyone who asks you, and if
anyone takes what belongs to you, do not demand it
back. Do to others as you would have them do to you.
(Luke 6:27–31)

Very few Christians would disagree that we should pray for
our enemies. But few of us consistently do it.

The word *enemies* can make us think of radical terrorist
cells or international leaders who hate America, and this is a
good place to begin in our prayers. Jesus's teaching applies to
enemies who wish to do us harm. But we can't stop there. What
about fellow Americans who actively oppose something you

care deeply about? What about those who disrespect your religious tradition? What about those on the other side of the political aisle who misrepresent and attack your political allegiances? Jesus's teaching applies to those who actively work against the ideas and beliefs you hold dear.

Let's take it deeper. What about a friend who violated your trust? What about a spouse who violated your marriage vows? What about a parent who violated his or her duty to protect and bless you when you were young? We all have been wronged in big and small ways, in formative moments and just yesterday. When people betray us, lie about us, deceive us, and fail to honor our friendship, we can act in ways that will deepen the conflict or we can follow Jesus's teaching to love and pray for them. (To be clear, loving an enemy does not necessarily mean staying in relationship with the person. Some people are dangerous, and wisdom invites us to act accordingly.) The genius of Christ is that we begin by praying for them, allowing God to heal our hearts and lead us to reengage them in a healthy way.

I struggled to forgive someone who was a constant source of frustration and hurt in my life. In fact, I found myself having imagined conversations in which I finally told the person off and, in so doing, "won" the battle. (The fantasy always played out like Tom Cruise and Jack Nicholson in the famous "You can't handle the truth!" courtroom scene from *A Few Good Men*.) After sharing this struggle with my spiritual director,

Father Michael, he taught me a simple forgiveness practice. Here it is:

- In God's presence, name to God all the things that bother you about that person.
- Pause and listen.
- In God's presence, name to God all the things that you imagine bother that person about you.
- Pause and listen.
- In God's presence, ask God to bless that person—his or her life, family, marriage, vocation, health, and so forth.
- Pause and listen.
- In God's presence, ask God to truly bless you.
- Pause and listen.

As Father Michael explained this practice, I could feel my heart slowly cracking open its door—excited about but afraid of this invitation. I told him I'd do this within the week, but he leaned forward and whispered, "Let's pray it right now." For just a moment, I considered hurling myself out the window into the nearby bushes and escaping back to my imaginary conversations. That's exactly what 1992 Tom Cruise would have done! But realizing that the window was locked and the bushes had thorns, I allowed myself to be led into the first step of blessing, forgiving, and loving this "enemy." Thanks be to God for wise guides such as Father Michael and for practices that help us join God's reconciliation of all things.

Start Small

You can't immediately heal the Israeli-Palestinian conflict. But if you are a Christian, you can reach out to a local mosque and build a friendship with a Muslim. We might not be able to instantly solve the racial divide in America, but we can commit to serving alongside one another in multiethnic, multicultural efforts. If you are passionately pro-life, you might not be able to overturn *Roe v. Wade,* but you can seek to help at-risk mothers who feel alone and afraid.

Many of us burn *so much* energy raging against big systems—Washington, religion, political elites, the culture, secularism, and more—that we never get around to doing much of anything. The scale of the problem becomes paralyzing. And if we're honest about it, raging against the system is a great place to hide. Pointing out the big people who cause injustice may be needed, but angry declarations are not the same thing as participating in the work of justice. Critiquing is not the same as swimming.

These things are easy to theorize about and much more difficult to do in real life. Let's now turn to a few concrete ways that our faith communities can start small as we join with God in God's work of redemption and the reconciliation of all things.

10

For the Sake of the World (Part 2)

Communities of Practice-Based Mission

I f you're anything like me, you often find the complexity and heartbreak of this world to be overwhelming. Even incapacitating. Our idealism compels us to step out of our comfort zones to try to help, but the brick wall of reality is not impressed by our good intentions. Cynics tend to be idealists who were disappointed one too many times.

Yet Christ invites us into the water. Not someday, but today. If we are going to learn to swim with Christ for the sake of the world, the time to wade in is now. But we can't do it alone. While the work must begin inside each of us, we can't join or sustain this work for any length of time on our own.

The crosscurrents of division and violence in the world and

in our communities are strong, and we need partners to swim with us in God's healing Current. Here are three ways that faith communities can do this.

OVERCOME THE FAMILIAR
US-VERSUS-THEM DEFAULT

We need to move from liturgies of *us versus them* to liturgies of *God's love for all.* Jesus came to earth not merely because God loved God's chosen people but because God loves the world (see John 3:16–17). I'm disturbed by the number of hymns and Christian songs that make use of war metaphors and position God on our side. To be clear, I do believe God is on our side as long as *our* means "everyone's." The Creator of every person on earth loves us all equally. There is no religious or cultural test that one has to pass before he or she is allowed to get into the River. All that is required is trusting Jesus enough to swim. God really is that gracious.

If you want to push deeper, we can build a biblical case that God supports some people while opposing others. But the people God sides with are not the ones we typically have in mind. God always defends the oppressed, never the oppressor. In Matthew 25, we see that Jesus aligns himself closely with the people who go hungry, those who are aliens in a foreign land, those who need clothing, and those who are sick or imprisoned (see verses 35–36). In fact, he goes so far as to say that whatever we do to them, we do to him (see verse 40). Christ is present in such people in a special way, so close is his identification with the oppressed.

The Scriptures also teach that God always sides with the humble, never with the proud (see James 4:6; Proverbs 3:34). But it must be noted that this support is based on actions, not on belief systems. The oppressed—as a category of people—do not make up a religious group, an ethnic group, or a nationality. "The oppressed" refers to any person who is being oppressed. Likewise, the oppressor is not defined by political allegiance, net worth, or heritage. Instead, "the oppressor" refers to the people and unjust systems that press down on those who are most vulnerable. The God of the Bible always is bent toward the oppressed.

Despite the special relationship God cultivated with Israel, God opposed God's chosen people when they were guilty of injustice and blessed them when they chose to do justice. (To explore these themes more deeply, read *The Prophetic Imagination* by Walter Brueggemann.)

Those of us who try to swim with Christ need to ask, "Do our liturgies (songs, prayers, and practices) help us see God's work in the other, especially those on the outside or underside of power, or do they deepen the us-versus-them narrative that reinforces the idea that we are right and 'they' are wrong?" Think through the last couple of sermons you heard. Notice the words of your church's favorite songs, readings, and prayers.

Take an honest, searching look at the liturgical practices of your community of faith.

John A. T. Robinson, in his book *Honest to God,* wrote,

> The test of worship is how far it makes us *more sensitive* to "the beyond in our midst," to the Christ in the hungry, the naked, the homeless and the prisoner. Only if we are *more likely* to recognize him there after attending an act of worship is that worship Christian rather than a piece of religiosity in Christian dress.[1]

Develop Liturgies of Comfort and Discomfort

We need liturgies of comfort and liturgies of discomfort. When we look at Jesus's ministry on earth, we see the many ways he brought comfort and grace and the many ways he brought confrontation and challenge. He didn't approach ministry with a one-size-fits-all approach, and neither should we. To the woman caught in adultery, he said, "Neither do I condemn you" (John 8:11), and showed her unprecedented grace. In contrast, he called a group of religious leaders "hypocrites," "whitewashed tombs," "snakes," and a "brood of vipers" in danger of hell (Matthew 23:27, 33).

Or consider the interaction Jesus had with Zacchaeus, a widely acknowledged sinner and cheater of his own people.

Jesus honored him by graciously becoming a guest in Zacchaeus's house (see Luke 19:5–10).

Contrast this with the way Jesus spoke to Peter, one of Jesus's closest disciples. Peter was a fiery, passionate man who at times lacked impulse control. Jesus forcefully said to him, "Get behind me, Satan!" (Matthew 16:23). And the Pharisees thought being called vipers in danger of hell was harsh.

Jesus approached people as the deeply loved daughters and sons they are and offered the word each needed. Jesus was the master at comforting the afflicted and afflicting the comfortable. He held his priestly role and prophetic role in holy and constructive tension. I believe that church communities, if we truly are following the way of Jesus, will do the same. A church that is about grace only, making comfortable people feel more comfortable, is telling only half the story. And a church that is about confrontation and attack without mercy is a dangerous place indeed.

LISTEN TO THE OTHER IN ORDER TO LEARN

It's important to create space in our gatherings (and in our lives) to hear the voice of the other. We don't listen to people in order to form counterarguments and defend our tribes. We listen to learn. In many circles, we're allowed to listen only to preapproved leaders, teachers, and others who adhere to a vetted list of beliefs and priorities. Some will learn only from those with whom they already agree. But if we cut ourselves off from everyone who believes differently, then we cut ourselves off from hearing anything that could teach us something new. What a loss! No wonder the divisions in our faith and world continue to deepen.

What if Protestants made more room to learn a sacramental theology from Roman Catholics and Eastern Orthodox Christians? And what if the white church made room to learn how to both lament and truly celebrate from the minority-culture church? (Pastor and jazz theologian Robert Gelinas's book *Finding the Groove: Composing a Jazz-Shaped Faith* is a brilliant meditation on what jazz can teach us about life and faith.)

And what if men made room for women to flesh out the other half of God's character and image rather than conform to the overly masculine image of God that we dudes have been presenting for millennia? And as much as I want to help stretch those in my own tradition, white evangelicalism also has something to bring to the party. Our bias toward action and focus on personal engagement can be powerful gifts to other traditions and to the world. But we learn only if we're listening. We must actively create space for hearing other voices.

To learn from people who differ from you, consider inviting teachers from different Christian traditions to teach out of the richness of their traditions in your church gathering. Also, delve into books and resources from a wide range of perspectives. Invite underserved and marginalized members of your community to share their stories and experience. Finally, embrace and include art from different cultures and traditions.

Gloria Anzaldúa (1942–2004) grew up in the mixed cultures of the American-Mexican border, which fueled the brilliant insights of her most famous book, *Borderlands/La Frontera*. May we have ears to hear and hearts to learn from her deep and hard-won wisdom:

> It is not enough to stand on the opposite river bank,
> shouting questions, challenging . . . conventions. A
> counterstance locks one into a duel of oppressor and
> oppressed; locked in mortal combat, like the cop and the
> criminal, both are reduced to a common denominator of
> violence. The counterstance refutes the dominant culture's
> views and beliefs, and, for this, it is proudly defiant . . . but
> it is not a way of life. At some point, on our way to a new
> consciousness, we will have to leave the opposite bank, the
> split between the two mortal combatants somehow healed
> so that we are on both shores at once and, at once, see
> through serpent and eagle eyes. . . . The possibilities are
> numerous once we decide to act and not react.[2]

WHAT ABOUT THE CHURCH AND POLITICS?

In response to the rise of the religious right starting in the late 1970s, some American Christians decided that political discussions have no place in church, while others married their faith to a political party. One group withdrew from the world, while the other became overly fused to it. I believe that both of these approaches have done harm to the church and harm to the world.

If the church is not *political,* it is irrelevant to the world that God so loves. But if the church is *partisan,* it becomes a tool of the power structures.

Being political means we are engaged in how society is organized. If we want to love our neighbors, we will naturally get involved in building systems that lead to flourishing and we will fight to change the unjust systems that target the poor, weak, and marginalized. We can't pretend to love our neighbors while we ignore the systemic realities that hurt them.

But the moment we tip into wholesale support for one party against the other, we take our eyes off our neighbors and join the system as apologists for only half the story. No political party is fully aligned with God's kingdom, and we need to find a way to engage the full reality of society without selling out to one side.

This is incredibly difficult, and I'll be the first to say that I don't do it perfectly. But we can't give up. The world desperately needs a brave and humble "third way." May God be gracious as we stumble forward—three steps forward and two steps back—into humble and meaningful engagement with the world that God so loves.

Over the last four years, our community has wrestled with ways to do this well, and we are stumbling forward together. Let me share one of the moments.

Prophets and Priests

In 2017, the Practice gathered two days after Donald Trump's inauguration as president. Our community included a few strong Trump supporters, a number of passionate Trump resisters, and many people in between. But nearly all of us were lamenting the ugliness of the political discourse. We wanted to work toward a way to engage constructively. We all desired to be instruments of peace, but we didn't know how.

As our team created the liturgy for the following Sunday, we decided to embrace two of the church's callings: to be priests and to be prophets. Not *either/or,* but *both/and.* We asked our favorite priest, Father Michael Sparough, to write and present a priestly prayer for President Trump. Using the Beatitudes, Father Michael led us to pray for our president, his family, his policies, and the flourishing of our country under his leadership. In this way, Father Michael helped us honor the teaching of Romans 13, 1 Timothy 2, and 1 Peter 2 in humbly supporting and praying for our leaders.

Following the priestly prayer and a few moments of silence, Claudia Lopez Heinrich offered a prophetic prayer she had written for President Trump. In the tradition of the Hebrew prophets and her own Latina culture, Claudia lifted a prayer that spoke truth against injustice and called Donald Trump to turn from his divisive language and actions and to turn toward the path of truth, justice, and kindness. We followed the two prayers by standing and praying the Our Father together. It was a beautiful, stretching, deeply holy experience.

A Benediction of Sorts

Gilbert Bilezikian is a legend in the Chicago area. Born in Paris in 1927 to Armenian refugee parents, he served in the French army and then moved to the United States to teach theology. In the 1970s, he had a student at Trinity Evangelical Divinity School named Bill Hybels, who later would flesh out Dr. Bilezikian's vision for the local church as Hybels helped form the Willow Creek Community Church and movement.

After returning from the Middle East a few years ago, one of my friends asked Dr. Bilezikian, "Dr. B., what do you think would happen if Jesus walked into Jerusalem today?"

The eighty-five-year-old educator, theologian, and mentor to many closed his eyes for a moment and finally whispered in his thick French accent, "Jesus would probably do now what he did then: take care of the poor, speak truth to power, and get himself killed."

May we go and do likewise.

Benediction

A Call to Reimagine and Reintegrate Everything Through Memory and Imagination

A great and mighty River flows throughout history toward the healing and restoration of all things. God has not given up on this world and invites every one of us to join this Eternal Current. Jesus showed us the way of the kingdom—fleshed out through the Beatitudes and resulting in the fruit of the Spirit on earth—and every person alive is invited into this redemptive flow. Can you see why they call it "good news"?

Yet, as we have seen, Jesus doesn't say, "Believe about this good news." The invitation is not to agree with the River or defend the River or write books about the River. The invitation is to join Christ and swim with the Current of God for the sake of the world. Regardless of what we believe, pray, or declare, if we're standing on the shore, we're missing out on the abundant life that is truly life (see John 10:10; 1 Timothy 6:19).

No matter who you are, where you've been, or how long you've been avoiding the River, Jesus is standing waist deep and calling to you in this very moment:

> Are you tired? Worn out? Burned out on religion? Come to me. Get away with me and you'll recover your life. I'll show you how to take a real rest. Walk with me and work with me—watch how I do it. Learn the unforced rhythms of grace. I won't lay anything heavy or ill-fitting on you. Keep company with me and you'll learn to live freely and lightly. (Matthew 11:28–30, MSG)

So here you are, listening to Jesus calling you to a baptism that terrifies and delights you. Could the invitation really be as good as it sounds? Or maybe you felt as if you had already answered the invitation, but now you realize you were simply splashing around in the shallows. You feel stuck.

What will you do? What should you let go of, and what do you need to hold on to as you wade deeper into the Current?

Or maybe you've been bruised and broken from being dragged across the rocks of religion. Maybe your only experience of water felt like drowning, and you wonder whether the way of Jesus can be trusted.

Friend, you are not crazy. You are not alone. And you are invited. No matter where you are coming from, there is a way forward. It is a path of memory and imagination.

MEMORY AND IMAGINATION

Without memory, we pull up anchor and drift with the winds of the moment. We refuse to learn from people who came before us, and instead, we repeat their mistakes. Without memory, we submit to the tyranny of the moment and lack the wisdom and tools to move beyond it.

We see this in stylistic fads and fast-food spirituality, in which most ideas are driven by popularity and the quest for efficiency. A friend who was a music director at a church for twenty years jokingly commented that the church's motto was "Never do the same thing once." An overemphasis on the new—pursuing innovation (at its best) and chasing novelty (at its worst)—will keep us trapped in the shallows. We rarely stay in one stream long enough to find the deeper Current.

As Spanish philosopher George Santayana famously wrote, "Those who cannot remember the past are condemned to repeat it."[1] The wisdom and treasures of those who have gone before us are an indispensable gift and protection for anyone on a journey. We need memory to anchor us in what always has been true.

But memory is not enough. We also need imagination.

Without imagination, we let our history tether us to a world that is quickly passing away. We freeze time in an idealized past and protect our homeland at all costs. Without imagination, all we can see is what we've already seen. We are merely a continuation of yesterday, which sounds very similar to the definition of despair: the belief that tomorrow can be only an extension of today.

In the Broadway musical *Hamilton,* one of the lead characters, Aaron Burr, wrestles with the disappointment of a life that has failed to meet his expectations. He follows the rules and plays it safe, but Burr keeps losing out to Alexander Hamilton, who neither obeys the rules nor plays the game. In the song "Wait for It," we see regret and resentment beginning to surface. Aaron Burr sings about his highly respected parents leaving him nothing but "a legacy to protect."

There are few things more crushing to kids than to feel that the purpose of their lives is merely to protect someone else's legacy. My wife and I, after listening to "Wait for It" for the millionth time, recently committed to each other, *Let's never leave our kids with a legacy to protect—like a huge weight around their necks. Instead, let's be a springboard that launches them into becoming the exact people God created them to be. May that be our legacy.*

When I was about eight years old, I was walking with my dad in our backyard and proudly announced, "Dad, when I grow up, I want to be *just* like you." More than thirty years later, I can still see the loving way he looked at me with a twinkle in his eye as he replied, "Aaron, I hope you're ten times the man I am." Now *that* is a springboard legacy for a kid. My dad may never know the imagination that his response unleashed in my heart and the holy possibilities it opened in me. Yet we don't always find those voices in our spiritual lives. Without imagination, our faith is merely a legacy to protect.

What if God's work in our past is not a legacy to protect so much as a springboard to launch us into the continuing story of God? There is profound continuation, of course, as we stand on the shoulders of giants, building on where we've been. But there is also wild and uncharted territory ahead for every one of us.

We must embrace and live into this dynamic tension: the humility of memory and the courage of imagination, the safety of memory and the risk of imagination, the continuity of memory and the possibility of imagination. And while it's tempting to choose one against the other, like nearly everything, the answer is both/and.

PRACTICES OF MEMORY AND IMAGINATION

So how do we live this out? Since the invitation of Christ is not merely to believe, what are the practices of memory and imagination that help us swim in our everyday lives?

In college I studied music theory and composition. One of my favorite professors, Dr. Paul Satre, used to remind his students that "you need to learn the rules before you can break them." We'd complain about learning another Bach sonata when all we wanted to be was the next Radiohead (this was the nineties). But Dr. Satre taught us that if we immersed ourselves in the genius of the classics, they would empower us for a lifetime of innovation. Repeating Bach was never the goal. But without learning from Bach, all we would do is repeat Radiohead.

I suspect that a practice-based faith is similar. We need to learn the rules before we can break them. (Or in my case, go back and learn the rules I've been breaking for years.) Formative practices, liturgies, and spiritual disciplines have been handed down through the generations, and it's a gift to learn from this collective wisdom. The goal is not to turn back the clock and repeat an earlier Christian era; the goal is to be carried forward by God's eternally present River. But studying and learning from those who swam with God throughout history form and equip us for a lifetime of innovation and exploration. A strong and informed memory propels us into bold and robust imagination. But both sides need to be cultivated.

In my journey as a low-church Protestant, the historic liturgy has been an incredible gift. Submitting to the shared memory of the great tradition is deepening and transforming my life from the inside out. But I have to keep reminding myself that it's not about historic liturgy or ancient practices and worship styles. It's not about structure or institutional approval or the fad of the moment. It has always fundamentally been about spiritual formation. What are the practices—ancient and new—that form us into Christlikeness for the sake of the world? What are the practices—of both memory and imagination— that help us swim in God's Eternal Current?

Would you consider that question for a moment? In your life, what practices do you sense God nudging you toward?

First, what is one practice of *memory* that can anchor you to the great story of God throughout history? How can you continue learning from the wisdom of those who swam with God before you?

A few examples: Read classic Christian books. Study church history or theology. Invite an older Christ follower to have lunch with you and learn from him or her. Attend a church that follows the historic liturgy. Choose from among the classic spiritual disciplines.

Second, what is one practice of *imagination* that will open you to the new things God wants to do in and through you? How can you clear space and make freedom for new life to be born?

A few examples: Read new Christian books. Experiment with fresh spiritual disciplines or even make new ones. Explore cross-disciplinary prayer (if you're great with words, opt for praying instead through painting). Learn about Christ through someone from another Christian tradition or even from another faith. Start something that didn't previously exist.

For the next thirty days, submit to one discipline of memory and one discipline of imagination and see what God does in you. Don't try to do everything at once—simply discern a next step with God and commit to taking it every day for a set period of time. I know from experience that God can do so much even when I offer God so little. All our loving Creator requires is that we crack open the door. God delights in unleashing a holy waterfall of blessing and healing.

A Life Immersed in God

When all is said and done, the spiritual life is not about practice; it's about God. We've focused on the central metaphor of swimming with Christ in God's River. But the River is what ultimately matters. It's not about perfecting our swimming techniques, as if our arms could cause the Current to move even for a second. The call of Jesus is to do anything and everything to get ourselves caught up in the River that has been flowing before us, is flowing now, and will keep flowing after all of creation is put back together.

You can do this in all your brokenness and glory. You really can. You can swim with Christ in the River of God for the sake of the world. And not just in church or from within the safety of holy spaces. You can learn to discover God's Eternal Current flowing in every moment, every conversation, every work deadline, every belly laugh, every moment of doubt, every fight with a spouse, every meal with loved ones, every funeral procession, every playground, and everything in between. For it is in God that "we live and move and have our being" (Acts 17:28). Wherever we go, we discover that the Creator and Animator of all life is already there. We cannot *not* be fully submerged in the presence of God.

Through a practice-based life, we can learn how to swim with Christ in the Eternal Current. Grace opened our eyes, grace invited us in, and grace will teach us the concrete ways to say yes, moment by moment, over and over. Thanks be to God.

ONE FINAL PRACTICE

So rather than ending this book with another idea to believe, I humbly leave you with a practice and a prayer. This might sound a little weird, but would you join me in a five-minute Examen on your experience while reading this book? Please don't miss the opportunity to notice what God has been doing in you. I'll guide you through it.

(Place both feet on the floor, open one hand as a physical sign of openness to God's Spirit, and take a deep inhale and slow exhale.)

Opening prayer: *Holy Spirit, please guide me in the next few minutes. Please grant me eyes to see your fingerprints and ears to hear your voice. Please speak. Your servant is listening.*

(Allow thirty seconds of silence to pass as you become aware again that you are already fully in God's presence.)

Reflection: As you look back over your experience of reading the book, what did you sense God doing and saying? Spend a moment thanking God for speaking to you and, above all, for inviting you to swim with Christ in the Eternal Current.

(Allow time to thank God.)

Reflection: What did you find helpful and encouraging while reading this book? What will you specifically integrate into your life? What did you find confusing or unhelpful about this book? What should you simply set aside?

(Allow time to hold these prayers before God.)

Question: How would you articulate the invitation God is extending to you today?

(Write God's invitation in the margin of this book.)

Finally, as we look forward to the future in hope, please join me in this prayer:

Eternal Creator and Lover of all you have made, thank you for life, breath, and the invitation of Christ to get swept up in your work of healing and restoring all things.

In this moment, I say yes to your Eternal Current. I say yes to the kingdom of God. I say yes to your un-forced rhythms of grace for the sake of the world. Please teach me how to swim. Please receive me, in all my brokenness and glory, and teach me to swim.

I pray this humbly and boldly in the name of the Father, the name of the Son, and the name of the Holy Spirit.

Amen.

A Note from Aaron

We believe that Sunday is not the main event of a spiritual life. But a church gathering can be a holy springboard to participate with Christ all week long. In a similar way, we're hoping that this book will help launch you into the next season of your practice-based faith. The invitation truly is participation.

A team and I have been working hard to create a series of resources, next steps, and liturgies to support your journey. You don't have to do it alone.

It's all available at www.aaronniequist.com.

For those who want to live a practice-based life, we offer a handful of resources such as

- practical steps to help you go deeper in specific practices like the Examen, centering prayer, the four steps of forgiveness, and so forth
- recorded liturgies to turn your car or living room into a sanctuary of practice
- resources to keep learning about and exploring the theology and daily experience of a practice-based faith

For pastors, worship leaders, and those leading in a faith community, we offer a handful of resources such as

- specific, hard-won lessons for how to bring liturgy and spiritual practices into a modern, nonliturgical church
- downloadable liturgies and specific resources to use in worship gatherings
- video examples of how a practice-based gathering can look in multiple settings

And because this is an ongoing journey for all of us, we'll continue to update the site with new resources, new liturgies, and new tools for individuals, families, small groups, and churches.

You can do this.

You, your actual self, with your actual community in your actual town. You can learn how to swim with Christ for the sake of the world.

We're honored to help in any way we can.

Grace and peace,

Aaron

Acknowledgments

First, I want to thank the Practice team (Steve, Rhianna, Kellye, Mindy, Lori, John, Jenna, Jason, Curtis, Sam, and Lisa) for all we experienced and learned together over the last four years. To say it was a communal effort is both cliché and absolutely true. Without the brilliant team, the Practice would still be a theoretical idea in a notebook. You each brought your incredible gifts and passions to this crazy experiment and fleshed it out in ways none of us would have imagined. And more than what we produced, the process of being on a team with you really shaped me. You were not just colleagues but sisters and brothers on the journey, and I couldn't be more grateful for you.

To the whole Practice community, thank you for jumping in with courage and grace. Thank you for being kind and patient with the organic and messy process. Thank you for bringing passionate hearts and open minds to every Practice gathering. Thank you for your prayers, words of encouragement, and willingness to rearrange your lives in order to put Christ's words into practice. A few of us launched an eighteen-month experiment, and you quickly turned it into an actual community. Thank you from the bottom of my heart.

I'll never forget my final Practice gathering with you in

June 2017. I pretty much smiled and/or cried for ninety straight minutes. It was a beautiful night to celebrate an incredible four years and to remind one another of all the ways God had helped us discover unforced rhythms of grace. Not perfectly. Not completely. But truly and sincerely. The experiment had worked beyond our deepest dreams. God was kind enough to do immeasurably more than we could have imagined, and we have begun to find our way in the Eternal Current. Praise God from whom all blessings flow.

Second, thanks to the Willow Creek leadership for allowing the Practice to exist. And not just merely allowing—you funded and blessed our experimental journey. Thank you for creating space for something like this to happen inside the Willow family.

Many thanks to Andrew and the WaterBrook team for believing I had something to say and then helping me say it. The first draft I sent to Andrew was an unmitigated disaster, yet he leaned in and patiently helped me craft my ramblings into something so much better. I love what this book has become, and I'm grateful for Andrew's clarity of vision, perseverance, and optimism throughout this whole process.

Thanks to my agent, Chris, for wisdom and talking me down from hundreds of ledges.

Many thanks to Angela, Steve, and Shauna for entering into the process at the eleventh hour with honesty and grace. The book wasn't working . . . and you helped us turn the corner.

To my bro, Eric Niequist, for standing in freezing-cold water for an entire afternoon to shoot the cover photo. You are the master. I'm so proud to see the goodness you're creating through New Branch Films. And thanks to Brittany and Blaine for assisting!

To Father Michael, Mark Scandrette, Ian Morgan Cron, Ruth Haley Barton, and the many other brilliant mentors who have influenced my life and ministry in a billion ways. Your fingerprints are all over this book.

And to the hundreds of fellow journeyers whom I have met along the way. Thank you for reminding me that I'm not crazy and I'm not alone. And neither are you.

Notes

Introduction

1. Martin Luther King Jr., quoted in John Craig, "Wesleyan Baccalaureate Is Delivered by Dr. King," *Hartford Courant,* June 8, 1964.

Chapter 1: Losing My Religion and Finding the Kingdom

1. Wikipedia, s.v. "Plymouth Brethren," last modified January 18, 2018, 09:55, https://en.wikipedia.org/wiki /Plymouth_Brethren.

Chapter 2: The Birth of the Practice

1. Our team was small, including Steve Carter, Rhianna Godfrey, Kellye Fabian, Mindy Caliguire, Lori Shoults, and a few others.

2. For more on this, see Simon Sinek, *Start with Why: How Great Leaders Inspire Everyone to Take Action* (New York: Penguin, 2009).

3. For more on this, see James K. A. Smith, *Desiring the Kingdom: Worship, Worldview, and Cultural Formation* (Grand Rapids, MI: Baker, 2009).

4. For more on this, see Dallas Willard's writing on spiritual practices in his book *The Spirit of the Disciplines: Understanding How God Changes Lives* (San Francisco: HarperSanFrancisco, 1991).

5. From the set of guidelines used at the Practice to set forth what practice-based faith consists of.

Chapter 3: Swimming with the River

1. N. T. Wright, *Surprised by Hope: Rethinking Heaven, the Resurrection, and the Mission of the Church* (New York: HarperOne, 2008), 184.

2. Wright, *Surprised by Hope,* 192.

3. Wright, *Surprised by Hope,* 193.

4. John Ortberg, *The Lord's Prayer: Praying with Power* (Grand Rapids, MI: Zondervan, 2008), 20.

5. Richard Rohr, *Everything Belongs: The Gift of Contemplative Prayer,* rev. ed. (New York: Crossroad, 2003), 29.

6. Brother Lawrence, *The Practice of the Presence of God* (New Kensington, PA: Whitaker, 1982), 24.

7. Do you have a godly spiritual director? If you want to learn more, I highly recommend you explore this Spiritual Directors Network: https://evangelicalspiritualdirectors network.com/home.

8. T. S. Eliot, "The Dry Salvages," in *Four Quartets* (Orlando, FL: Harcourt, 1971), 39.

9. If you want to explore the Examen more deeply, check out "A New Liturgy No. 6: The Examen," a recorded thirty-minute liturgy that Father Michael Sparough and I created, www.anewliturgy.com/no-6-.

Chapter 4: Church as a Gymnasium (Part 1)

1. M. Robert Mulholland Jr., *Invitation to a Journey: A Road Map for Spiritual Formation* (Downers Grove, IL: InterVarsity, 1993), back cover.

2. To explore the practice and theology of spiritual formation, a good place to begin is https://renovare.org.

3. See James K. A. Smith, *You Are What You Love: The Spiritual Power of Habit* (Grand Rapids, MI: Brazos, 2016).

4. John Witvliet, conversation with the author, July 23, 2013.

5. "Confession of Sin," *The Book of Common Prayer and Administration of the Sacraments and Other Rites and Ceremonies of the Church* (New York: Church Publishing, 1979), 79.

6. John Perrine wrote a short paper titled "The Story of Practice Throughout the Scriptures" specifically for this book. So very helpful! The rest of the paper is posted at www.aaronniequist.com. He recently finished his MDiv at Trinity Evangelical Divinity School and will eventually

pursue a doctorate of theology. He played a central role on the Practice leadership team (2014–16) and currently works full time in the discipleship department at Willow Creek Community Church.

7. Barbara A. Holmes, *Joy Unspeakable: Contemplative Practices of the Black Church* (Minneapolis: Fortress, 2017), 19.

8. Sandra Van Opstal, "Sandra Van Opstal on The Next Worship," interview by Joan Huyser-Honig, Calvin Institute of Christian Worship, April 7, 2016, https://worship.calvin.edu/resources/resource-library/sandra-van-opstal-on-the-next-worship.

9. For more on this, see Sandra Maria Van Opstal, *The Next Worship: Glorifying God in a Diverse World* (Downers Grove, IL: InterVarsity, 2016).

10. Ian Morgan Cron, "Prayer," June 9, 2011, video, 4:43, www.youtube.com/watch?v=qYHLwAIDxtM.

11. Thomas Keating, *Open Mind, Open Heart: The Contemplative Dimension of the Gospel* (New York: Continuum, 2002), 136.

Chapter 5: Church as a Gymnasium (Part 2)

1. Paraphrased from a quote in "Barth in Retirement," *Time*, May 31, 1963.

2. Ian Morgan Cron (sermon, the Practice, South Barrington, IL, June 1, 2014).

3. David E. Fitch, *Faithful Presence: Seven Disciplines That Shape the Church for Mission* (Downers Grove, IL: InterVarsity, 2016), 26.

Chapter 6: Sunday Is Not the Main Event

1. To read the story of Martin Luther's conversion to *sola fide,* see Roland H. Bainton, *Here I Stand: A Life of Martin Luther* (Nashville, TN: Abingdon, 2013), 50–51.

2. Dallas Willard, "Kingdom Living," interview by Andy Peck, May 2002, www.dwillard.org/articles/printable .asp?artid=92.

3. Peter Scazzero, "Session 8: Go the Next Step to Develop a Rule of Life," Emotionally Healthy Spirituality Course, DVD transcript, www.emotionallyhealthy.org/wp-content /uploads/2017/11/EHS-Course-DVD-Transcripts-2017 -.pdf, 2.

4. Ruth Haley Barton, "Interview with Ruth Haley Barton Regarding Sacred Rhythms," Transforming Center, July 28, 2011, www.transformingcenter.org/2011/07 /interview-with-ruth-haley-barton-on-sacred-rhythms.

5. Dallas Willard, *The Spirit of the Disciplines: Understanding How God Changes Lives* (San Francisco: HarperSanFrancisco, 1991), 56.

6. Richard Rohr, "Nothing Is Excluded," Center for Action and Contemplation, June 17, 2015, https://cac .org/nothing-is-excluded-2015-06-17.

Chapter 7: We Need Everybody

1. Richard Rohr, *Everything Belongs: The Gift of Contemplative Prayer,* rev. ed. (New York: Crossroad, 2003).

2. David G. Benner, *Human Being and Becoming: Living the Adventure of Life and Love* (Grand Rapids, MI: Brazos, 2016), 118–19.

3. "3625. oikoumené," Bible Hub, http://biblehub.com /greek/3625.htm.

4. John Armstrong, conversation with the author, March 9, 2016; see also John H. Armstrong, *Your Church Is Too Small: Why Unity in Christ's Mission Is Vital to the Future of the Church* (Grand Rapids, MI: Zondervan, 2010), 32.

5. Margaret Rose, "What Is Ecumenism . . . and Why Does It Matter?," November 11, 2013, video, 2:46, www.youtube.com/watch?v=xMAQb2DyWVI.

6. Ian Morgan Cron (lecture, New York City, March 27, 2015).

7. See "The Learning Pyramid," https://siteresources .worldbank.org/DEVMARKETPLACE/Resources /Handout_TheLearningPyramid.pdf.

8. Richard Rohr, *Immortal Diamond: The Search for Our True Self* (London: Society for Promoting Christian Knowledge, 2013), xxii.

9. Pope Francis, "Pope Explains Ecumenical Dialogue," February 26, 2017, video, 2:30, www.youtube.com /watch?v=gLjHKbyc_r4.

Chapter 8: We Can't Do It Alone

1. Eugene H. Peterson, *Under the Unpredictable Plant: An Exploration in Vocational Holiness* (Grand Rapids, MI: Eerdmans, 1994), 17.

2. Peterson, "Spirituality for All the Wrong Reasons: Eugene Peterson Talks About Lies and Illusions That Destroy the Church," interview by Mark Galli, *Christianity Today,* March 4, 2005, www.christianitytoday .com/ct/2005/march/spirituality-for-all-the-wrong-reasons .html.

3. N. T. Wright, *What Saint Paul Really Said: Was Paul of Tarsus the Real Founder of Christianity?* (Grand Rapids, MI: Eerdmans, 2014), 116–17.

4. Soong-Chan Rah, *The Next Evangelicalism: Freeing the Church from Western Cultural Captivity* (Downers Grove, IL: InterVarsity, 2009), 153.

5. Rah, *The Next Evangelicalism,* 144.

6. Mindy Caliguire, conversation with the author, February 12, 2014. See also her book *STIR: Spiritual Transformation in Relationships* (Grand Rapids, MI: Zondervan, 2013).

7. David Augsburger, *Caring Enough to Hear and Be Heard* (Scottsdale, PA: Herald, 1982), 12.

8. "3-Way Listening" and many other resources available at www.onelifemaps.com.

9. Dietrich Bonhoeffer, *Life Together* (Minneapolis, MN: Fortress, 2015), 75.

10. Bonhoeffer, *Life Together,* 92.

11. Ronald Rolheiser, *The Holy Longing: The Search for a Christian Spirituality* (New York: Image, 2014), 83.

12. Information from Jerusalem Greer is used by the express permission of Jerusalem Greer. All rights reserved.

Chapter 9: For the Sake of the World (Part 1)

1. "Our Story," Telos, www.telosgroup.org/who-we-are.

2. "About," Gravity, https://gravitycenter.com/learn /about.

3. Phileena Heuertz, *Pilgrimage of a Soul: Contemplative Spirituality for the Active Life,* rev. ed. (Downers Grove, IL: InterVarsity, 2017), 186.

4. Bethany Hoang, "Deepening the Soul for Justice: An Interview with Bethany Hoang," interview by Laura Merzig Fabrycky, The Washington Institute for Faith, Vocation, and Culture, July 2, 2013, www.washingtoninst .org/5355/deepening-the-soul-for-justice-an-interview -with-bethany-hoang.

5. See Richard Rohr, "Community as Alternative Consciousness," Center for Action and Contemplation, April 19, 2016, https://cac.org/community-alternative-consciousness-2016-04-19. His exact quote is "Remember, *how you do anything is how you do everything.*" (Italics in the original.)

Chapter 10: For the Sake of the World (Part 2)

1. John A. T. Robinson, *Honest to God* (London: SCM Press, 1963), 90.
2. Gloria Anzaldúa, *Borderlands/La Frontera: The New Mestiza* (San Francisco: Aunt Lute Books, 1987), 78.

Benediction

1. George Santayana, *The Life of Reason; or the Phases of Human Progress,* vol. 1, *Introduction and Reason in Common Sense* (New York: Charles Scribner's Sons, 1917), 284.